GRIEF'S WALKING STICK

A PERSONAL JOURNEY FROM SORROW TO SERVICE

FEATURING THE SEVEN LANGUAGES OF SORROW

REVEREND STEPHEN L GARRETT

FriesenPress

One Printers Way
Altona, MB R0G 0B0
Canada

www.friesenpress.com

Original cover concept by: Daina Deblette— Professional Artist, Teacher, Counsellor and Coach, Salt Spring Island, British Columbia, Canada / www.dainadeblette.com

ISBN
978-1-03-831434-5 (Hardcover)
978-1-03-831433-8 (Paperback)
978-1-03-831435-2 (eBook)

Social Science, Death & Dying

Distributed to the trade by The Ingram Book Company

Why This book?

Well, I'm a pretty ordinary guy, a baby boomer—one of nine million in Canada—raised in a world that, over the past dozen decades, has become avoidant of death and grief in a big way—understandable, given all the death my parents' generation experienced from World War I through the Spanish flu pandemic, right into the Great Depression. Since the early 1900s, death has found its way from the family home to the hospitals, while funerals have turned from a family and neighbourhood event to a funeral business. Now that it is in the hands of professionals, we all seemingly have washed our hands of the "dirty" business of death and grief; my family was no exception.

My baby boomer upbringing regarding death and grief was painfully common. My family, all seven of us, simply didn't talk about "it." We kept a stiff upper lip when death and grief showed up on our doorstep. We gave into the fear the image of the Grim Reaper had created. It didn't seem to matter much whether it was a person or pet that died; they were here one day and never spoken about the next. It was as if they had never existed. All in all, life and death, it seemed to me, were simply taken for granted. They both had become no big deal; it was all just kind of matter-of-fact and ordinary.

Oddly, this approach of avoidance and denial seemed to have worked. My family and I were able to keep death and grief at bay. When death did come knocking, we simply handled it and got back to life without even skipping a beat. It looked from the outside that we were able to move through these challenging end-of-life issues with grace and dignity. Fantastic, yes?

Hmmm, not really. We avoided "it" like the plague. We all seemed to store our emotions away in some dark, hard-to-find closet—way at the back, of course. We were totally dysfunctional regarding the grief process, from active dying to death to grieving. In fact, so were most of our family's friends and my own colleagues and pals. Interestingly, we were so accustomed to being in denial of it all, we didn't even notice that we were. We all lived a kind of half-life, a life that lacked the inspiration and urgency an inspiring teacher named Death could provide.

This book is about my personal and intimate journey from a world of death and grief denial to a world of its embrace. An adventure that saw me turn my personal sorrow into service for others. A kind of how-to manual for the regular guys and gals wanting to do death and grief differently, with more heart, more thoughtfulness, and more spiritually. It's a book you will hopefully find full of encouragement, inspiration, and practical spiritual wisdom. Timely, too, given the mass exodus of the baby boomer generation coming quickly toward us over the next decade or two.

This book is dedicated to my sister Jody, who died in 1988, my father, Lloyd, who died in 2004, my brother, Peter, who died in 2015, and my mother, Marge, who died in 2022.

Your living and your dying has a profound effect on my growth and evolution as a spiritual human being.

I love and miss you all deeply.

Table of Contents

A Wake-Up Call I Could Not Ignore
Cracks in the Foundation of Denial

It was the late in the day on May 5, 1988.

It was a Thursday.

I found myself in downtown Toronto, working for Burns Fry Limited, living in a brownstone townhouse on Shuter Street with my then fiancée. I was fully engaged in the matrix we call the American Dream. Life was full of parties, work, sporting events, some travel, and, yes, more and more work. There was nothing wrong in my life it seemed, at least not on the surface. I had recovered from my earlier nasty divorce and was now ready to do it all over again with a new partner. I had a solid career, a few good friends, and some money in the bank. I was looking forward to life in the fast lane.

Looking at my life from the outside, you'd get the idea that I had it all together—a good job, a good partner, a good home, and a good family. Everything seemed good! Seduced by the apparent goodness of my own life, I hadn't realized how much more deeply I had actually fallen asleep since my first marriage ended in a type of nasty death we call divorce. I had totally surrendered to the mistaken beliefs that had me living a life that Garrett men typically led. Much like the character Neo in the movie *The Matrix*, I didn't even realize I was actually sleep-walking through my life on some sort of weird pre-programed auto-pilot.

And so, it was—that is, until the unexpected happened.

I was heading home after a full day at the office followed by a squash game at the Adelaide Club and a quick bite to eat at a local downtown café. It was closing in on 9:00 p.m. when I opened the door and stepped inside my second-floor apartment. The telephone was ringing off the hook in that kind of urgent way, as if someone really needed to talk with me.

I answered the phone. It was Roy, my sister's husband, calling from St. Catharines, Ontario, where they lived. Roy said, "Jody is gone," to which I responded cavalierly, "Where to, Mexico?"

Roy couldn't answer. He passed the telephone to his mother, who said, "Jody died tonight at 6:30 p.m. We haven't called your parents yet. Could you?"

Stunned into an almost total numbness and a sense of duty as the eldest child, I said, "Sure," and hung up. Looking at my fiancée, I said, "We have to go to Mom and Dad's. Jody just died."

From that point on, I don't remember much about the drive or our conversation along the way, if there was one. In those moments, it felt as if I was running strictly on autopilot; everything seemed just a little outside my grasp, like I was in some kind of weird impenetrable bubble of numbness.

When we arrived at my folks' place, it was late, closing in on 10:30 p.m. I rang the doorbell, and Dad greeted us with a baseball bat in hand, just in case some weirdo showed up at the door, I guessed. As I stepped into the foyer and the door closed, I blurted out, "Jody just died." Dad was stunned. We went upstairs and gave Mom the news too. What I do remember is that shocked look on both Mom's and Dad's faces when I told them what had just happened. They each responded tearily, "It should have been me."

I recall little else until the day of Jody's funeral ceremony, though I do remember little bits of the funeral home gathering, the viewing, and Jody lying dead in a casket. I recall sitting in the room where Jody's casket lay on display, struggling with the idea of going up to the casket and seeing her dead body. Part of me didn't want to, as it would make it too real. A deeper part of me, though, knew intuitively that I needed to see Jody one last time and say my goodbyes. So up I went and stood silently by her side and cried my wordless goodbye to her. It was her body no doubt, yet it didn't feel like her. Something was missing that I didn't have a name for at the time.

The church service was followed by the burial, and it all happened right around Mother's Day on Sunday, May 15, 1988.

I was a pallbearer, one of six friends and family members who would carry Jody's casket from the church to the hearse and then on to the gravesite. I can only remember little glimpses of the whole scene, such as the hundreds of people who gathered to pay Jody their final respects. I recall my father encouraging me not to cry and to keep a stiff upper lip. I remember the minister speaking from the front of the church; it was all mumbo jumbo to me, and I couldn't make sense of anything he said. I remember the weight of the casket as we carried it from the church to the hearse, and the dread I felt as we walked with Jody's casket in hand toward her gravesite and final resting place.

At the gravesite, the numbness I'd been experiencing all week suddenly vanished. Life instantly became crystal clear the moment we began slowly lowering Jody, in her casket, into her grave. Hand over hand, we all slowly, carefully, and lovingly lowered her down until the casket made a disturbing thud as it hit bottom. In that moment, that very instant, it seemed as if a switch in me turned on. I became fully alive and present like never before. It was as if someone had powered me up. I was turned on like a neon light bulb.

Jody was dead. I was alive, and none of it made any damn sense to me.

In that timeless instant of presence and clarity that only death can bring, I made a commitment to my dear dead sister Jody—I would discover the meaning of life and death and make some sense of what had just happened. I intended to know the truth about both life and death, and I meant it!

Though I was deep in sorrow over the loss of my dear sister Jody, somehow, I knew in my heart my life was about to change in ways I could never imagine. Though not clear to me in the moment, my journey from sorrow to service, though in its infancy, had just been birthed as had the notion of Grief's Walking Stick.

You will notice that a great walking stick is simply just there in the umbrella stand at the front door. It doesn't draw any attention to itself as it waits patiently to be picked up and taken on its next adventure. When returned to the umbrella stand, it simply sits there as if it never left. The humble walking stick knows itself and its role and serves when it is chosen.

No big deal. The walking stick is serving just by being available and ready to be chosen.

Section One
Turning Away from Death:
How I Learned to Banish Dying, Death, and Grief from My Life

Setting It All Up

I was born to Marge and Lloyd Garrett on October 22, 1949, and raised in Montreal, Quebec, at a time when the fabled Montreal Canadiens went on a five-in-a-row Stanley Cup run. Back in those days, there were only six teams in the now thirty-two-team National Hockey League.

Things were different back then, shortly after the Second World War. Television was just finding its way into the family rooms of North America. The suburbs were taking a foothold and beginning to squeeze out the farmers. At the time, there was no worldwide internet; that began in 1983. There were no cellphones, not until 1988. Social media? Nope, not until Facebook and Twitter launched in 2004 and 2006 respectively. It was a digital-free world back then.

In 1949, the annual salary of a Canadian man was $2,900.00. A new car cost $1,420.00, a home $7,450.00, and a gallon of gas 17 cents. A loaf of bread was 12 cents, a dozen eggs 24 cents, and a hot chicken pie fetched 20 cents. The North Atlantic Treaty Organization (NATO) was formed, Newfoundland joined Canada as a province, and the Montreal Alouettes won the Grey Cup.

I had a pretty normal childhood it seemed, though we moved a fair bit as our family grew from three to four and finally stopped growing at seven of us. I was a pretty happy, playful kid with lots of friends and a keen interest in anything other than school. I went to Lakeview Elementary, played ball hockey on the street outside my house, and watched *The Ed Sullivan Show* and Walt Disney.

In my teen years, I smoked a little pot, illegal back then, and hung out at the "tree," a huge willow tree that was a gathering place in the woods for us teenagers. It was out of sight and granted us the privacy we all needed to explore our adolescence. I graduated from Lindsay Place High School in 1967 and went straight to work for the Bank of Montreal, 207 Hymus Boulevard Branch, Pointe Claire, Quebec, as a branch management trainee. I married in 1970, moved to Vancouver, BC, and continued my banking career with the late great Bank of British Columbia.

Unknowingly though, I was fully committing to living the American Dream. It seemed as though I was awake in my life, yet now looking back, I was so not! I was on autopilot, kind of going through the motions as I'd been taught to do by my family and the culture I lived in.

Building the Forms for the Foundation of My Death-Adverse Life

After World War II, Canada and Quebec, the province I lived in, moved into a time of economic prosperity of sorts. Baby bonuses were enacted to encourage the growth of families, and women were encouraged to leave the post-world war workforce, as free child-care and tax incentives were put in place to encourage it. The school system was standardized to ensure a literate society, and its students learned to fit in. School uniforms were part and parcel of the high school system back then: white shirt, grey pants, blue blazer, black shoes, and a tartan tie.

We were all being groomed to be law-abiding citizens of a modern society and, more importantly, to be on some sort of predictable path we now call the social clock. Fitting in was deemed decidedly more important than being your natural and somewhat rebellious, unique, and priceless self.

In my house, Dad ruled the roost, made the money, and called all the shots. The woman, my mother, dutifully enabled her husband and often, at least until the kids were grown, was a stay-at-home mother. There were five of us children: three sisters, a brother, and me, the eldest. We lived in the suburbs west of Montreal in a little town called Pointe Claire on the West Island. It was a full house. I had a comfortable life as a kid, yet, unknowingly since birth, I was creating a personal belief system that would run the first thirty-nine years of my life without interruption.

Pouring the Concrete

A lot went on in my family when I was very young, just a little boy. Things that had more to do with my mother and father working out their lives and their relationship. Stuff that made no sense to me was going on all around me. Parties, alcohol, fights, and lots of unexplained nonsense abounded. Of course, I took it all personally and made-up stories about myself based on what I saw, heard, and felt going on in my family home. Much of it was programmed deep into my subconscious from the time I was born until I was about six or seven years old. Most of it was feeling-based and not at all intellectual. I take exception with Rene Descartes who said, "I think, therefore I am." My personal experience is that I feel, therefore I am.

Next, the Framework

My teenage years were used to cement those feeling stories into thoughts, and those thoughts … well, I turned them into behaviours and habits that reaffirmed my personal belief system, mistaken though it was. By the time I turned twenty, my personal belief program, my personal matrix if you will, was running my life. I didn't realize I was not at all in charge.

The Structure Is Complete

The first two decades of my adult life was used to reaffirm all those self-created ideas of who I was and what I was worth, and I embedded these negative self-images even more deeply into my unconsciousness. By the time my first marriage came to a crushing end, I was fully committed to my mistaken identity. I was totally dedicated to my core beliefs, so much so that I thought they were the real me. The autopilot switch was locked into the on position; sound asleep, I was. Yet in a very real way, I had succeeded; all the necessary ingredients were now in place for my eventual awakening, bumpy and uncomfortable as it would be.

I recognize now that I had lost connection with my true self. I was sleep-walking through each and every day of my young life. I also realize now that being asleep was an important and necessary ingredient to my eventual awakening, which began in earnest on May 5, 1988.

The Topper—Death and Grief Denial

Regarding my upbringing around dying, death, and grief—to be honest, I don't have many clear childhood memories. My grandma died when I was three, my grandpa Joe when I was a young child, and that's about it. What I do recall, though, is that we never spoke about either one of those important deaths. As a matter of fact, we never spoke about the death of anything, even our pets; they just disappeared, never to be seen or spoken of again. My beagle, Sam; our favourite dog, Ginnie; and any number of birds, cats, and mice were there one day and gone the next. Vanished and banished, it seemed to me.

I vaguely remember being at the funeral home for Grandpa Joe's service. I recall asking a bunch of questions and getting no answers to any of them. It all seemed so weird to me at the time.

Grandpa Joe was in a box.

He had a tie on. He never wore ties.

His hands were placed across his chest and he was wearing makeup. What? His skin was cold to the touch.

It was suggested that I go outside with the rest of the kids. I had death nightmares for six months after his funeral. The hardest part was that I had no one to go to and talk with about death and the sadness I held in my heart for Grandpa Joe.

When I was a child around seven years old or so, I remember dashing into the house with a dead robin in my hands. I was excited and not the least bit scared. I wanted to check with Mom about where the robin went because it wasn't in its body anymore. Mom was upset and seemed shocked or angry. She grabbed the little robin from my hands, wrapped it in some toilet paper, put it in a paper bag, and threw it into the garbage can. Robin gone and never spoken about again.

I thought I had done something wrong.

Now that I'm thinking about it, I also remember that a few of my hockey teammates were killed in a car accident. Oddly, that was it. We didn't attend their funeral and never spoke about it after the fact. We all just carried on somehow with the games at hand and with our teenaged lives.

That's how it was done back in those days, at least in my family. It was all neatly tucked away in the closet, never again to see the light of day.

Looking back, it seems death and grief were the bad guys back then. I guess that makes sense given the end of the Second World War and all the suffering it brought, which was piled on top of the First World War and the Spanish flu pandemic, followed by the Great Depression. I imagine folks were simply overwhelmed by it all and wanted it all to magically go away somehow.

So, go away it did.

North America became highly death and grief adverse. As a culture, we banished death to the hospitals, and it was now a medical issue. We had our loved ones whisked away to funeral homes and let others handle the messy details of after-death care. We become passive voyeurs in a very real way, as if we could somehow avoid the messy topic altogether.

Here's a piece written by Kay Jonson that helps explain this phenomenon:

> In North America, death and grief are not spoken about readily or easily. In many families, children observe three

important, albeit flawed, life lessons: do not talk about death or acknowledge grief; be strong and put on a smile no matter what; and get over it and move on as fast as possible when someone dies. A powerful contributor to this death-denying phenomenon is the media. Not only does it publish the most appealing, dramatic details about a death, but it also focuses its advertising avalanche on being and staying young. By denying realistic end-of-life smells, sounds and physical changes, and the inevitability of ageing, the death experience is promoted as an unfortunate but temporary event that can be dealt with by using the right mouthwash or hair dye.

Deborah Carr adds:

> Throughout the late 19th and most of the 20th century, death became "invisible" (Aries, 1981) and "bureaucratized" (Blauner, 1966). Physicians and hospitals assumed control over dying, death and mourning became private, the handling of dead bodies and funeral rites were transferred from private homes to funeral parlors, and people were encouraged to deny the inevitability of death and stake their hopes on the promise of nascent medical technologies (Blauner, 1966). Treating dying patients in isolation was believed to help smooth the transition beyond death; reducing the social status of those who were about to die would minimize disruption of social and economic relationships.

Here are a few more comments about how we got ourselves into this death-denying culture of ours. They were written by Emma Reilly in a *Hamilton Spectator* article titled "In Denial About Death" back in 2011.

> Death lurks in the corners of our lives, threatening to emerge from the shadows at any moment. When it bursts into our day-to-day existence—sometimes unexpectedly, occasionally anticipated—it is almost always unwelcome.

In Canada and the western world, we have reached a point where we will do almost anything to convince ourselves that death doesn't exist. "Death is the last great taboo," writes Julia Samuel, a grief psychotherapist and founder patron of Child Bereavement UK, in her bestselling book "Grief Works."

"We seem happy to talk about sex or failure, or to expose our deepest vulnerabilities, but on death we are silent," she writes. "It is so frightening, even alien, for many of us that we cannot find the words to voice it."

But experts who work in the field of death and dying say our increasing tendency to ignore death, no matter the cost, is hurting us. Our death illiteracy means we are woefully unprepared to handle the growing number of aging people in our society, says Denise Marshall, associate professor of palliative care at McMaster University and the Medical Director of the Niagara West Palliative Care Team and McNally House Hospice.

The tendency to eradicate death from our everyday lives is also a relatively new historical development, Marshall added. Just picture any death scene in a historical movie or novel; the dying person is likely to be at home, encircled by friends and family, rather than in a hospital surrounded by doctors. It has only been in the past hundred years or so that death became so highly medicalized. Marshall dates the removal of family members from their loved ones' deathbeds to the 1920s—the same time doctors started to better understand the infectious nature of tuberculosis. "It's the first time in the Western World that health care said, 'You, the community, must stay out,'" said Marshall. "And so began the beginning of institutionalized death. It's not that long of a history."

By the end of the twentieth century, aging, too, was something to be avoided at all costs, as ageism took deep root in our culture. Dying and death were now fully the domain of the medical system, and funeral arranging had become big business at the cost of losing family-run funeral homes. We the people were now mere witnesses to the death process and vulnerable consumers for the corporate funeral businesses.

So, what to do with all this denial and avoidance? How can we bring dying, death, and grief back to everyday family life where it truly belongs, where it can inspire us all to live even more full and passionate lives? Well, all I can do is share with you what I did to move from denial to acceptance, from fear of death to freedom to live. It's a bit of a story, so let's begin!

Chapter One
The First Big Adult Loss
I Wasn't Yet Ready for a Wakeup Call

Pale sunlight,
pale the wall.
Love moves away.
The light changes.
I need more grace
than I thought.

— The Essential Rumi

In my adult life, my first big non-death loss was a divorce from my first wife, Lesley.

She and I were high school sweethearts. We met at Lindsay Place High and fell in love. Her family moved from Montreal to Vancouver when we were both in our final year of high school. That February, I ran away from home and hitch-hiked across Canada in the depths of winter to be with her! Yep, crazy puppy-dog love, it was. Froze my toes somewhere between Toronto and Winnipeg, and upon my arrival in Vancouver, I was rushed to the doctor for a look-see. Gangrene, it was, and after only three days with my sweetheart, I was flown home in order to get the medical care I needed. They saved all my toes—well, not quite true. I lost half the big toe on my right foot and was dubbed by my friends upon my return to school with a new nickname: Half Toe!

Lesley and I stayed in touch, and ultimately, she moved back east to Toronto, where my family and I then lived. She and I got married in 1970 and set out to create a family of our own. Things didn't go so well, and after an affair of Lesley's, we decided to move to Vancouver for a fresh start. Yeah! Hmmm, that didn't work out so well either. So, in 1977, after another extra-marital affair of hers and one get-her-back affair of my own, we divorced.

It was a nasty time for sure.

The death of my first meaningful adult relationship was a real test for me, and I didn't do too well. In fact, I failed to handle it at all. I headed home to Toronto for a little family support, and that was all I got—a little. My mother was sympathetic, and my dad simply said to go back to Vancouver and make it work. Neither one of them gave me any idea how to deal with the deep sadness and grief I felt as a direct result of the painful and unex-pected ending—the death of my marriage. In fact, I really had no idea that I even needed some professional help emotionally and mentally.

Most of my friends encouraged me to find someone new and get over it. "It's likely for the better" was a common piece of advice. So, I followed their advice and sucked it up, held it all together, and headed for divorce court!

I had no concept of what to do with all the emotions I was feeling as a direct result of this death. I was angry, sad, confused, numb, and stunned, to name a few of them. Nothing in my young life had prepared me for this unexpected and abrupt change. All I was taught as a child was to diminish my own feelings, to keep a stiff upper lip, and in no way to express my emo-tions. "For God's sake, don't share the family laundry with friends" was the message I heard rattling around in my head. It sounded like my dad's voice.

After a short period of internal struggle, I did what I was taught to do. I simply got on with my life and suppressed my emotions by tucking them away in a remote corner of my body where hopefully I'd never have to deal with them again. I hid them behind a mask of behaviours that had me looking like I had my shit together. I distracted myself with a slew of new girlfriends, a whole lot of partying, and overworking. All these distractions did their job, and I ultimately "forgot" what I experienced as a direct result of my divorce.

Case closed and neatly filed away never to see the light of day again, or at least, so I thought.

A Gem of Grief's Wisdom

What I know now in hindsight is that all my unexpressed thoughts and emo-tions were simply stored away in my mind and body. Tucked neatly away just beyond my awareness until such time as I would be ready to confront the hard truth of why this nasty divorce had come my way. Until then, I put on the happy face, ignored my feelings, and distracted myself with parties, girlfriends, and some pot. Oh yes, and I also overworked.

By the way, tucking it all away was only a temporary solution. It was all I could do in the moment; I knew no other way, yet it brought me only temporary relief. All that being said, in hindsight, I was simply delaying the inevitable confrontation with the reality of my own suppressed sorrow.

We often diminish non-death losses such as divorce because we simply don't see them as a death. Job loss, moving, and financial loss are a few other non-death losses that carry with them grief—a grief that is often disenfranchised.

Here is a simple formula to help you notice where grief stems from;

Death = Loss = Change → Grief

Chapter Two
Big Adult Loss Number Two
Opening to Death and Being Disturbed by It

> Let me respectfully remind you
> Birth and Death are of supreme importance.
> Time swiftly passes and opportunity is lost.
> Let us strive to awaken. Awaken!
> Take heed,
> Do not squander your life.
>
> — A Zen Evening Prayer

In the opening of this book, I told you a bit about the impact my sister Jody's death had on me. Here is a little bit more about our relationship and our family that may help you understand why her death hit me so hard.

By the way, I'm the big boy to the left of Mom. Jody is the blonde on Mom's righthand side. Younger brother, Peter, is on my right, and sister Susan is peering over my right shoulder. Carrie was yet to be born and would follow seven years later. We were a sweet, though somewhat dysfunctional, little family.

Jody and I were each other's favourite for whatever reasons. Though she was three years younger than me, we spent lots of time together as kids. As we moved into adulthood, Jody really blossomed. She worked for the Royal Bank during the day and volunteered her evening time to many non-profit organizations in St. Catharines, Ontario. She was particularly supportive of a women's shelter and devoted both her time and some of her money to their brilliant cause. I admired her social consciousness and was a little envious of her commitment to helping others. I was a Bay Street boy and focused mostly on making money for me. We were this interesting pair of seeming opposites, Jody and I.

She married Roy, an odd sort of biker fella with a big heart. I kinda liked him. He really loved Jody, so he was instantly in my good books. We would often spend time together on the weekends, drinking some of her rather bad coffee, playing some cards, and chatting lots about life and living. We all really liked each other and had lots in common.

Jody was born on December 23, 1952, so her birthday preceded Christmas by a slim two days. I always felt a little sorry for her, as she often got birthday presents and Christmas presents as a weird blended package. I would always buy her a special "birthday only" present to try and make up for it.

Our relationship was special to both of us. We were kindred spirits of sorts and really connected in the heart. We just loved each other for no particular reason. She saw me for who I was; I didn't have to put on a show for her. I could just be me, and Jody loved me anyway. Her love was a real and genuine gift to me!

And then all of a sudden, she died, with absolutely no warning or even a hint. My special love—gone!

It was most often unbearable in those early days right after her death. So, I did what I was taught to do as a young boy. I sucked it up and put on some kind of fake happy face. Though it appeared on the surface that I was doing okay, behind the many masks I wore, I was really deeply struggling.

Emotionally

I kept my emotions to myself. That didn't mean that I wasn't feeling; I was feeling deeply! I just didn't know how to name the feelings or how to express them. I was emotionally handicapped as a result of my upbringing and how I saw my parents, siblings, and extended family handle their emotions, which was not to handle them at all. The emotions I felt from Jody's death began mingling with all those pieces of stored-away grief from earlier in my life. It felt as if it was all just too much to hold.

13

Mentally

I just couldn't figure the whole thing out. Why Jody and not me? Why now, so early in her young life? Why would God let this happened? Why did all the rest of my family seem like they had simply breezed through it? Was I the only one thinking these thoughts? Was I a hot mess and the only one in my family to be this upset? Was I crazy?

Physically

It was a similar story. The power of all the emotions coursing through my body was incredibly disturbing, even though I didn't show it. I found ways to distract myself, though, to numb myself out, to avoid the emotions, to do anything but face my feelings. I would drink too much or smoke a little too much pot. I would eat some junk food. I would let my emotions come out as aggression on the hockey rink or the squash court. But the relief was always only temporary.

Spiritually

I was in way over my head. I had fond memories of my younger years in church. I sang in the choir. I was an altar boy, and I taught Sunday school to the younger children. There was something about the ceremony, the rituals, the fragrances, that I felt in some way deeply connected to. I couldn't put my finger on it exactly; it simply felt like home somehow. But, now with Jody's death, all this was up for review. God had somehow messed up, and I wanted some time with Her to set the records straight. I fully intended to give God a piece of my mind!

To sum up, I was truly a mess on all fronts, even though on the surface I looked as if I had it all together. Honestly, I needed help. I didn't know where to look for it or what kind of help to look for.

As happenstance would have it, one day about a month or so after Jody's death, a friend of mine said he was going to New York to do a men's workshop. *A what?* I thought. Yes, it was a men's personal development workshop called "Men, Sex, and Power" led by Justin Sterling. The next event was being held on June 18 and 19, 1988. My friend Keith simply said, "Oh come on, it can't hurt, and besides, I'll keep an eye on you."

So, I signed up and off I went to New York to take part in my first-ever personal growth workshop. It was just over a month since Jody's death. Little did I realize the significance of this: my first step on my spiritual healing journey. To be honest, I didn't even know that I was about to jump on a spiritual healing path. I had no idea what I was getting myself into, or perhaps I should say, out of.

I don't recall much about the two-day event. There were hundreds of other men there, lots of practices and exercises we were all put through, and Justin did a fair amount of ranting from the stage. It was a flurry of activity well into the late hours of Saturday. What I do recall, though, is the anger exercise Justin led us through on Sunday afternoon.

We were told to create a list of women we were angry with, and what we were angry about. Then in small groups of eight men, we were each given the opportunity to step into the centre of the circle and let our anger rip. One at a time, we stepped in, and one at a time, we did our best to express our anger to the men witnessing our rant. It all seemed fine in a way—that is, until it was my turn.

I nervously took my spot in the centre of the circle and started to yell at my first wife for being unfaithful and leaving me. Then before I could stop it, I began to yell at Jody!

"How could you just die like that? How could you not say goodbye to me before you left? How could you not tell me you loved me one more time?"

Then the raging screams surfaced, and I just yelled my angry ass off. When it was done, I fell to the floor and cried like I had never cried before. The circle of men bore witness to all of my emotions and, in a strong, masculine way, held space for me. No one tried to fix me, stop me, or lift me to my feet. They all just witnessed my rageful sorrow, and that was all I needed. A few of my witnesses were Graham, David, Paul, Rob, and Mark. To this day, I am eternally grateful for their strong, silent, collective support in my time of profound need and budding transition.

As quickly as the weekend began, it was over.

I was on a plane back to the Toronto Island Airport, returning to my nine-to-five life on Bay Street, or at least, so I thought. Once home in my brownstone and unpacked, I had a hunger for a vanilla ice cream cone, so off I went to the St. Lawrence Market to get one, a double scooper at that.

On my way home from the ice cream shop, fully enjoying my cone, I stepped off the sidewalk at Queen Street and Jarvis right into a transcendental otherworldly experience unlike anything I had ever felt, seen, heard, or experienced before. All of a sudden, the world around me seemed to freeze. I was the only actor on the stage of life that was moving in that moment.

It was the most unusual experience I'd ever had. It was if time stood still and the universe was speaking directly to me. I wasn't located in my body; it was a kind of out-of-body thing. It was as if I was everywhere and nowhere at the same instant. Time was non-existent. The only way I can describe the experience is to say: "I am the space between all things. I am the tick between the seconds."

It was a full-blown awakening. In that moment, I had no doubt that I had just experienced something profound—profoundly simply yet profoundly deep at the same time. I had no reference point for what I had just come into contact with. I was simply dumbfounded, and blissfully so.

Days later, I told my friend Keith of this odd experience, linking it to my grief and sorrow over Jody's death. Keith referred me to a counsellor friend of his who specialized in grief and all things spiritual. Judy, the counsellor, and I spent an evening a week together processing all my stuff, both emotional and spiritual. Though our working relationship lasted for a short three months, it was the gateway into a whole new way of experiencing the world, and it led me to a new circle of friends and fellow truth seekers. With Judy's help and support, I was able to lean into the deep grief of my sister's death; I was able to face it and express it. Instead of denying my grief, I accepted it and, with her help, worked with it.

Beneath the façade I wore, the cracks in my life's foundation continued to grow.

A Gem of Grief's Wisdom

The full expression of my grief for Jody's death and its reception by my men's team created a space, a kind of spiritual meadow, that was conducive to an awakening experience. Awakening can't be made to happen; however, my unsuppressed expression of grief around Jody's death tilled the soil in the new meadow I found myself standing in.

I had just learned that expression works so much better than its opposite: depression/suppression. Being with death in this authentic way opens doors for me to step through into my greater self.

Chapter Three
The Learning Begins
Recognizing I Am Actually Lost

Reflection is the beginning of reform.

— Mark Twain

I found myself in a new group of friends, and to me an unusual group indeed. They were all spiritual seekers of truth—an odd fit given the corporate life I was currently living in. Yet somehow, I felt so at home in this strange new world. I was challenged to reconcile the life of a corporate finance guy with this new life of a seeker of spiritual truth. And, as time went on, I became more and more curious about this new group of friends and more involved with enlightenment intensives and the Institute of Ability led by Charles Berner (aka Yogeshwar Muni). I threw myself into Berner's work, and through two of his students, Anjali Hill and Skanda (Lawrence Noyes), I began studying mind clearing, emotional trauma release, couples relating, and the enlightenment intensive process.

The more I studied, the more I realized how little I knew about living a life based on spiritual truths. I felt as if I were back in kindergarten! Yet I stayed with it and began staffing intensives whenever and wherever they were offered. I signed up for all the events Skanda was teaching in the Toronto area. Four-day, seven-day, and fourteen-day retreats all focused on discovering the answer to these four primary questions:

- Tell me who you are.
- Tell me what you are.

- Tell me what another is.
- Tell me what life is.

All intended to help me and many others discover and directly experience the truth of self, others, and life. More simply put—to wake up!

The more I explored this new world, the more it became clear that something needed to change in my life. The juxtaposition of corporate finance and spiritual life was untenable for me. I knew deep in my gut that I wanted to help people, not sure with what or how, yet the call to be of service to others beckoned.

So, for the first time in my life, I actually listened to and followed my heart. About a year to the day after Jody's death, I marched into my boss's office and told Mark that I was quitting the corporate finance business and moving to the West Coast with the intention of becoming a social worker. Mark's parting comment was something like this: "Well, you certainly won't make much money doing that!" It was a sign that I had made the right decision for me.

Dad and I worked for the same firm, Burns Fry Limited. We worked in the same department, bond and money markets, on the same floor, a mere ten feet from each other. Yes, I know. How the hell did that happen? The moment after I announced my resignation to Mark, I walked over to Dad's desk and sat down for a son-father talk.

"Dad, I just quit. I've decided to move to Vancouver and begin a new life," I said hurriedly. "I think I want to be a social worker or something like that."

"Son, I'm so proud of you," Dad said.

I was shocked. Dad was proud of me for quitting? I'd been searching for his approval my entire life, and now that I was stepping away from his world, he was proud of me. Like, what the heck? So, I asked him about it.

Lloyd responded with the wisest thing he had ever said to me: "Son, how could I approve of you being me? You're setting out to be your own man now. I'm so proud of you!"

This was one of the most special moments with my dad—a moment I will always fondly remember.

I was now committed to a new life. There was no turning back; I was moving west to British Columbia and leaving my old life behind at the corner of King and Bay streets. The impact of my sister Jody's death was very clear; in a spiritual way, I had been born again!

A Gem of Grief's Wisdom

More often than not, a mid-life crisis is a gift or an opportunity in disguise. This was the case for me. Jody's death, as devasting as it was, was also a doorway I chose to walk through. I wouldn't have said so at the time, yet in hindsight, it provided me with an opportunity to become more of the person I was born to be. The Hopi say that death is a place of choice between a dark rabbit hole or a portal; to this day, I'm not sure what encouraged me to choose the portal, but I'm glad I did!

Jody's death was an inspiration for me to live life much more fully. Her death was my wake-up call. It was a doorway into a new future I wouldn't otherwise have chosen.

Chapter Four
The In-Between, the Bardo, *the Gap*
Following My Opening Heart

The universe turns on an axis.
Let my soul circle around a table
like a beggar, like a planet
rolling in the vast, totally helpless and free.

— The Essential Rumi

Having sold everything, including my status mark Ford Merkur XR4Ti, I packed what were my necessary belongings into the burgundy GMC van I affectionately called Bud and left Toronto heading west, ultimately to British Columbia's Sunshine Coast, where my new life was destined to begin.

I remember a moment as I was driving through Northern Ontario when I was simply driving my van and happily whistling. I can't recall a time prior to this feeling so truly free, happy, and footloose. It was a remarkable moment, to say the least.

I was untethered, unshackled, and free of all the chains that had previously bound me to a life that no longer served me. I was deeply happy in my heart. It was as if my life was now perfect somehow. That feeling stayed with me all the way to the Sunshine Coast, where my life as a social worker was about to begin. First, though, I had a home to build for my new family, and Brigit and I needed to find our way around a whole new community and learn an entirely new lifestyle. I was no longer an urban dweller; I was a rural kinda country fella.

To get started, I took a job as a dock-boy for Wally Nowak, the owner of Fisherman's Resort. I purchased an acre of land on Garden Bay Lake and began building my new life. I designed the family home, hired Ted Woodard to build it with me, had two kids, and worked my ass off in my new community, ultimately becoming the interim executive director of the local Community Health Council. I volunteered my time to a number of non-profit societies, ran for public office, and was totally committed to doing things for others in the form of community service. I was living a new, more authentic version of me.

Interestingly, and unknowingly of course, I began falling asleep again, though in my new and different life. My new life, the new me, slowly became a mask behind which I hid. The falling asleep process took about seven years, and I didn't even notice that it was happening again. Gradually, I lost touch with what had woken me up in downtown Toronto only a few years earlier. Though the spark of my first awakening never left me, I had forgotten to tend to it and keep it alive in me.

Yes, I had changed. And, yes, my life was good, rich with friends, work, passions, and dreams. Building a home, a family, and a brand-new lifestyle was all so much fun and so rewarding. I was living a life truer to my deeper heart's calling, and it felt good. I felt more like me, and I was much more engaged in my life. I was a different fellow than the one who had awoken at the corner of Queen and Jarvis.

It seemed as if I were just getting more comfortable, more at home in my new life, and more relaxed being a father with two young sons. All that emotional stuff that woke me up when Jody died now was resting somewhat dormant in the hidden caverns of my body.

The comfort was seductive and sleep inducing. It was much like the story of the frog in a bucket of water that was slowly brought to a boil, and the frog boiled to death unknowingly. Yet that same frog, if dropped into the same bucket of already boiling water, would immediately hop out! I was the frog and my life was the boiling pot, and I was fully immersed in it.

Little did I know that I was sowing the seeds for another wakeup call. Another non-death loss, one that would propel me into yet another remarkable lifestyle change. Another spiritual awakening, one that would have me step even more fully into a newer and deeper version of me.

A Gem of Grief's Wisdom

Falling asleep seems to be a fundamental part of waking up. We seem to do it spiritually with a fair bit of regularity. We have an awakening moment, a spiritual aha. We pay attention to it and then seemingly fall asleep again but in a new phase of our ever-evolving life. My big aha in Toronto landed me in a new phase of my life and catapulted me across the country to begin all over again, it seemed.

Chapter Five
Divorce Number Two—Big Loss Number Three
So It Was Me All Along

> *That's why we need a great deal of courage to challenge our*
> *own beliefs.*
> *Because even if we know we didn't choose all these beliefs, it is*
> *also true we agreed to all of them.*
>
> — Don Miguel Ruiz, *The Four Agreements*

I will always remember the evening it happened. I had organized a birthday party for my then wife Brigit at Ruby Lake Resort, and a fine event it was. Most of our friends had shown up, and all were having a grand time, me included. It was in this party atmosphere that Brigit decided to announce her intention to leave me and take up life with another fellow.

Boom.

In one moment, one instant, one breath, my entire life exploded into smithereens. As the plot unfolded, I found myself an outsider in my new life. I left the family home I had built, moved to a small cabin in Sechelt, and became a weekend dad and very much a recluse. It was stunning, shocking, and hard to swallow how my life had changed so dramatically in just one moment. The uttering of a few little words had sent my life into another seeming tailspin.

At the same time that my marriage came to a crashing end, my employment contract was terminated due to budgetary concerns, so I was also without income. I was struggling with several non-death endings and full of all kinds of emotions, ranging from confusion to anger to sadness to numbness to rage and despair. Everything I had identified myself by was gone: my relationship, my family, my home, my job!

Embarrassed and ashamed of myself, I began to hide away in my little hovel of a cabin. I seldom went to town and rarely went outside. I felt so ashamed of where I found myself again. Such a failure. I just couldn't face my friends. I dropped deeper into my well of sorrow and isolation. This time facing death, I chose the rabbit hole, and spiraling down it I went.

Now a hermit, alone with my crazy monkey mind, I hid out, only seeing my two dear boys on the weekends. Isolated, a slave to my crazy thoughts, I festered feeling all alone, betrayed, and oh so sorry for myself. I felt victimized. I fleetingly thought of ending it all, and had it not been for my two young boys, perhaps I might have. Then one Friday late afternoon while all these crazy thoughts were pouring though me, Oliver and Ben were being dropped off by their mom. This thought sobered me up out of my "poor me" stupor: *Is this what I want to teach my boys? When the going gets tough, quit?*

No! was my immediate answer.

Once we had the boys' backpacks in the cabin, the three of us headed to downtown Sechelt. It was the first time in over three months I had gone to town. Partly out of necessity, and partly to step back into my life, it was all I could think of doing. I had no money or any food in the house; penniless, I was! Broke and seemingly broken, I decided to stop at my favourite restaurant: the Mother Earth Café. I was surprised by how warmly we were greeted by Brian, the owner and head chef.

"Hey, Stephen, where have you been? The hot chocolate is on me!" he chirped warmly. I was immediately relieved by both his warm greeting and his generosity.

Brian delivered the drinks to our table, and I followed him back into the kitchen. I needed to fess up. "Brian, you need to know that I'm broke, unemployed, and have no food for the boys this weekend. I'm lost and don't know what to do," I said, full of tears and emotions.

Brian looked straight at me and said, "No worries, Stephen, dinner is on me."

Relieved that I had Friday night handled, I went back to our table and joined the boys. Brian showed up several minutes later with burgers and fries for us and placed dinner in front of the two boys. As they dug into their food,

Brian slipped $100.00 cash into my top pocket and said, "Starting Monday, you're my new dishwasher!"

Brian's kindness helped me jump back into my life and begin living again. I was the best darn dishwasher ever to step foot into Mother Earth Café! I was so grateful for Brian's generosity. I worked with Brian and his team for a year, and most happily so. I gradually came back to life and began again. This time, though, I chose to look at things differently. I was done with the blame game. I was done being a victim in my own life.

"Who's in charge of my life anyway?" was my guiding question as I struggled to make sense of my tattered world. Much as I did with Jody's death, I decided to use the "death" of my second marriage as a catalyst for my growth and development as a spiritual human being. It was easy to blame people in my life for all my losses and failures, yet the blame game wasn't changing the trajectory of my life. I simply kept looping through my life in rather obvious and habitual patterns. As I continued with this life review of sorts, it became humblingly obvious that I was the common denominator in my relationships, my social networks, and my work life. Blame was no longer an option! It was all me! In order for me to live freely, my blame game had to die.

In order to change my life, to renovate it, I needed to first take full responsibility for my life. A tall order for sure, yet in doing so, I found the key to my own personal freedom. Using the death of my sister, the death of my careers, the death of my relationships, the death of my identities, and the death of my homes as compost, I was able to reclaim my personal power and begin to drive my life forward. Using my grief and loss as opposed to hiding from them, I was able to slowly reclaim the steering wheel of my own life's car.

Jody's death had a profound positive affect on my life and, in a way, prepared me for the next steps in embracing my life by befriending all the "deaths" I had suffered. Now that my eyes had been re-opened, I was able to see more clearly that I was the creator of my own universe. Death was actually inspiring my personal evolution—the deaths and losses I experienced were the very fuel propelling me forward in my living a more heart-centred life. I was beginning to turn more fully toward death, loss, and grief; they were slowly becoming dear, encouraging friends. This time, I realized I needed to face my grief demons. I was coming face-to-face with all the hidden grief from all the losses I had not fully experienced or expressed over the years.

Now was the time to turn toward death and grief and invite them into the light of my days.

A Gem of Grief's Wisdom

As tough as it was to do, the act of taking 100 per cent responsibility for my life was the key to my personal freedom. It unlocked the cell door I had built around myself for my own protection; I was my own jailer, and unexpressed grief formed my jail cell bars.

Chapter Six
The Messy Middle
Back in the In-Between, the Bardo, the Gap

The mystery does not get clearer by repeating the question,
nor is it bought with going to amazing places.
Until you've kept your eyes
and wanting still for fifty years,
you don't begin to cross over from confusion.

— The Essential Rumi

Buddhists refer to the space between a death and a rebirth as the bardo, or the gap, in between an ending and a new beginning. This is where I found myself again—in the in-between. I was looking back at my life and all the deaths I had experienced, and looking forward to a future I had yet to design for myself. I was in between my relationship with death. I wasn't afraid of it any longer, yet I hadn't fully turned toward it and embraced death as the inspirational teacher it truly is.

I was taking stock. What had I learned since my sister's death? What had I learned from my relationship deaths? What did I learn from the death of my career? What do I want more of in my life? Less of? What was grief teaching me? What was death inspiring me to do? What had life taught me about myself, my thoughts, my personal beliefs? What can I let go of that is no longer working for me?

Tons of questions! And, in the moment, no clear answers. Ah yes, patience. Sitting in the gap, the bardo, takes patience; the truth and learning cannot be hurried. So, I gave myself lots of time with no pressure to get my life together by a particular date. I did set the intention that I would reinvent myself based on my life review. I did get a journal in which I could record my answers. I put up a poster board in my cabin titled "The New Me and My New Life," on which I stuck tons of Post-it notes.

Then I simply settled into answering all the questions I mentioned above. It took time—days, weeks, months, and years. I stayed with it, though, and in its own time, my new self-identity and new life began to take form. As the answers became clear, I put them into play in my new and evolving journey.

What I didn't realize then but know now is that this process of sitting in the gap and doing a life review was the beginning of a life-long practice, not just a one-off exercise.

Here are some results of my first life review:

- ✓ I stayed in social work, as it was and still is a core value of mine.
- ✓ I went to Royal Roads University and earned a master's degree in leadership.
- ✓ I attended to the needs of my two sons.
- ✓ I continued to explore spirituality and my work with the Institute of Ability.
- ✓ I stayed active as a hospice volunteer.
- ✓ I continued writing poetry.
- ✓ I continued to eat well and exercise.
- ✓ I continued to explore what worked for me and what didn't.
- ✓ I allowed my heart to take the lead more often.

I had recognized through all of this that I had found the right ballpark— social service, or more accurately put, being of service to others. Now that I had found the stadium, it was a matter of finding the right section, the right row, and ultimately my own seat.

I knew I was in the right place, and all I needed to do was pay attention. I completed my master's degree while working for the local health council. I spent time in the social services field as an executive director and a frontline worker. I continued to pay attention to how I felt when I was doing what I was doing and to make adjustments as I moved along. I felt better working with people on the frontlines as opposed to running an agency.

I moved around a bit and worked in rural communities and larger urban centres and finally settled in Vancouver, BC. I hadn't found my seat yet, but I sure knew the section of the stadium that suited me—working face-to-face with people in a way that would support and encourage them to be all they could be. I wasn't yet at my final resting place—my own seat—but I sure was closing in on it. I reminded myself often that time was not the issue. Persistence, patience, and purpose would get me to my seat.

It was now 2003.

An entirely new chapter of my life was about to be written.

A Gem of Grief's Wisdom

Personal growth takes time, discomfort, perseverance, willingness, and ongoing support. All five ingredients are necessary to break through the layers and masks we've built around ourselves in order to protect our sensitive yet unbreakable hearts.

Chapter Seven
Jumping into the Deep End
A Spiritual Dream—Right Stadium, Wrong Row

> *The Dream you are living is your creation. It is your perception of reality that you can change at any time. You have the power to create hell, and you have the power to create heaven. Why not dream a different dream?*

> — Don Miguel Ruiz, *The Four Agreements*

After years on the Sunshine Coast, my second painful divorce, and a decade of education and training and job exploration, I found myself reconnecting with my friend and teacher Anjali. She had another student who was in the midst of setting up a personal growth company he called WarriorSage. He was looking for a few people to work with and help him build this fledgling, personal spiritual growth company.

The opportunity spoke directly to my heart: helping people grow spiritually. I was all in! So, in early 2003, I left my social work job in Vancouver's downtown east end and headed to WarriorSage to begin yet another new chapter of my life.

During this period of time, my dad died. It was in the winter of 2004. I had flown back to Toronto, where Mom and Dad lived. Dad was very sick in the hospital and on life support, as all his major organ were failing. After I arrived at Lester B. Pearson Airport, I went straight to the hospital and met Mom there. At the age of seventy-eight, Dad was close to taking his last breath.

Mom and I hugged, said our hellos, and were immediately faced with the attending doctor, who asked, "Well, what should we do?"

I kind of thought that was the doctor's job, so I said, "What do you mean?"

The response was rather clinical, and as he went into how Dad was plugged into a life support system and all that medical jargon, I went kind of brain dead. My family never had talks like this before, yet here Mom and I were, in a hospital hallway outside my dad's room, being expected to do just that. I clumsily asked the physician for some time and space so Mom and I could talk privately and freely.

We looked at each other in this kind of "here we go" way and just started to talk about what we thought Dad would want. We'd never discussed this with him, so we had to do our best and simply guess. Dad was pretty limited in what he could do during this time of his illness. No cribbage, no golf, no sports on television. His friends wouldn't stay visiting more than a few uncomfortable minutes. None of his favourite foods, and away from his home and comfortable routine. I assumed he wasn't particularly happy in his life. Mom and I agreed on this and came to a difficult yet heart-based decision. Take Dad off life support.

He died hours later. When he died, I noticed a weird sense of relief coursing through my body and heart.

The funeral home viewing and the church funeral were reminiscent of Jody's. Lots of friends and family, lots of stories, some tears, some more stories, and it was all over, it seemed.

My relationship with Dad had been a little bumpy over the years, and the more he drank, the bumpier it got. I remembered a time when I actually laid the law down with Dad. He was getting sloppy when he drank, slurring his words and looking old and haggardly. I told him that if he wanted to spend time with my family, his two grandkids, he would have to be stone-cold sober. My sisters did the same thing, and Mom too. So, he stopped, and for the next few years, we actually had Dad back! Then his health began to deteriorate and we lost him again, this time to the medical system. Though not to a bottle of vodka, we still lost him. As the Beatles once sang, it was a long and winding road.

I flew home and got back to my life with WarriorSage, suppressing my feelings still, though this time not so vigorously. It was more like managing them as opposed to stuffing them down.

I really had no idea where this personal development company was going or how I would fit into the small family-run business; after all, I had most often worked for larger organizations. That being said, I knew in my heart it was going to be a most fun and unusual ride, and it did not disappoint. As things moved along at WarriorSage, I met my current wife, Sonora; she and I grew as a couple and also as a teaching couple within the company. Sonora also became a vice president and assumed a role as the owner's right-hand woman.

We were a workshop company and began giving workshops in Canada similar to Peak Potential and the Harv Ecker gang. We offered introductory workshops; Sex, Passion, and Enlightenment, a relationship workshop; The Illumination Intensive, a spiritual awakening workshop; and added others as we grew and evolved. We created The Path of the WarriorSage and Spiritual Adventure Tours as time went on.

To provide a bit of background, I had been studying with Anjali and Skanda and had trained to be an enlightenment master, a mind clearer, and an emotional release therapist, so I had the exact background needed to support WarriorSage. Over the years, I advanced in my skills and abilities and took over leading the workshops listed above. I became the vice president of Training. It was a truly exciting time in my life, and I got to do things and visit places I wouldn't have otherwise seen or done.

We gave workshops in Western Canada; Seattle, Washington; and San Francisco, California, to name a few locations. Our reputation grew, as did our audience, our students, and our following. We began to offer Spiritual Adventure Tours and travelled around the world with groups of senior students to places like Egypt; Tulum, Mexico; Machu Pichu in Peru; Kenya, Africa; and Europe and Britain. For me, most impactful were our trips to India and cities such as Bodh Gaya, Varanasi, and Allahabad. Not realizing it in the moment, my visits to India were to have a profound effect on my life as I continued to grow and evolve.

Things, though a little crazy, moved forward as the company grew in size and stature. We were successful financially, our reputation as a training company grew, and we were flat out busy. Yet the seeds had been sown and things started to go off the rails, as is often the case with these New Age, spiritual growth companies. There is a tendence to become a bit cultish, and so did we. In 2011, along with other training companies, there was a big shake out, and WarriorSage was not excluded.

I won't go into all the internal details, but suffice it to say, it was not pretty, and in early 2012, I took my leave. My wife and I left the company we had helped to build.

Another death, and this one hurt my heart deeply. I went from a full-on trainer/facilitator to the ranks of the unemployed. From travelling the world and training people to the confines of my home in Walnut Grove, BC. I was numb and stunned. Even though I had made the choice to leave, it was still a significant non-death loss.

For months, I just stumbled around trying to find myself. I was so identified with WarriorSage, my role there, and my love of what I was doing, I no longer knew who or what I was. I had lost track of me again and now needed to reinvent myself. I needed to find a new path, a different way to serve. It felt like another total renovation of my life.

And it was.

A Gem of Grief's Wisdom
Have those difficult end-of-life conversations way before you think you need to. Being planned and prepared makes those difficult decisions a little less so. Thanks to Dad's death for this lesson.

Notice all the non-death losses too, as they are profound teachers if we choose to look at them in that way. Things don't happen to us; they happen for us!

Section Two
Turning toward Death:
Learning How to Embrace Dying, Death, and Grief

Chapter Eight
Big Loss Number Four
The Spiritual Dream Dies—What Now?

> *What you can do, or dream you can, begin it now.*
> *Boldness has genius, power, and magic in it.*

— JW von Goethe, *Faust*

So, WarriorSage and I had parted ways after a decade-long journey of spiritual service. Now what? Yep, back in the bardo, the gap. Interestingly, though, I was beginning to value this in-between space; it was a time of deep personal reflection.

As is the case with all changes, losses, or deaths, there are always gifts hidden in the minutia of the details of the experience. This was certainly the case for me and the end of my personal training career. So, instead of ignoring my recent death, I chose to lean into it, review it, feel it, and look for the lessons and gifts it had for me. I chose to turn toward the pain and the grief of the loss of all I once was.

When I did, the gifts became apparent. As I reviewed my time with WarriorSage, I started to see that I had developed some great interpersonal skills, some solid leadership abilities, and the capacity to work with people on a spiritual level. I had memories of remarkable experiences. I recalled many moving conversations. My time in India on two spiritual adventure tours was particularly memorable, moving, and inspiring, as were my experiences in Cairo, Egypt, Peru, the Serengeti, Kenya, Tulum, Mexico, and a number of other spiritual hot spots.

As I thought about all I had done and experienced in India, I began to get a sense of what was important to me that was hidden in the depths of my heart. I recalled my time in Varanasi. The memories were clear as a bell, as if I was actually reliving them, particularly my time at the ghats on the banks of the Ganges River, where funeral pyres burnt in full public view. Varanasi is known as the City of Death, a place where many Hindus want to go to be cremated on the banks of the Ganga River.

I spent a week there just sitting on the steps near to the Shiva Fire. I watched with amazement the ceremonies that unfolded in front of me: the community feel, the public acceptance of these most beautiful death rituals, the full involvement of all family members. It was beautiful, breath-taking, and oh so not the way we did death back home.

Families would carry their loved one on their shoulders down to the banks of the Ganga River and place them carefully and lovingly on the funeral pyre. The eldest male family member would then take a torch up to the Shiva Fire, from which all funeral pyres were lit. The story goes that this fire had been burning nonstop for over five thousand years. There was a firekeeper, a yogi, who tended the fire and kept it burning day and night. It was a sacred and noble job, I was told.

One day as I was leaving my favourite seat on the steps, this amazing yogi beckoned me to join him by the fire. I spoke no Hindi and he spoke no English, so we had to rely on hand gestures, body language, and facial expression to communicate. He had me sit down by the fire close to him.

We simply just sat there in silence, as if in some kind of meditation.

Then he began to put ash from the fire on my face and wrists. He was chanting as he performed this ash ritual. He then wrapped up some ash and handed it to me with so much love in his eyes, I was overcome with joy. It was as if something had shifted in me. It was a most memorable and sacred moment.

I also recall my time at Machu Pichu and deep in the jungles of Peru, and the impact the Peruvian culture had on me—sacred ayahuasca ceremonies with my late friend and teacher Diego del Palma, and the teachings of the snake, condor, hummingbird, and puma. The snake represented subjective experience—belly to the ground. The condor represented objectivity—clear vision from above. The hummingbird was the messenger between me and my higher power. The puma was the result of the balanced approach of both subjective and objective perspectives—right action. The condor feather I was gifted with symbolically sealed the lessons of their spiritual power symbols. The feather has a sacred place on my altar.

This lesson was so impactful, it found its way onto my right thigh as a tattoo!

There was the time I spent in Tulum, Mexico, with Don Jorge, and all the otherworldly experiences I stumbled into amongst the Mayan ruins. I felt as if I were living the life of Carlos Castaneda. Don Jorge didn't disappoint; he taught me how to shape-shift, a skill that has served me and those I serve so beautifully well. In the New Age growth world, the expression used instead of shape-shifting is "to feel into" the other person. Don Jorge taught me how to apply this shape-shifting technique for the sacred service of others.

Not to forget the late Hakim in Cairo, Egypt, and my experiences there inside the great pyramids in the Kings' Tomb, or my journey up the Nile to the Valley of the Kings. Yes, even more moments of profound and deep spiritual teachings of truth. Oh, and then there was my time on Kenya's Serengeti and the remarkable presence of the magnificent animals who were so gracefully allowing me to visit their home, and the Masai and their amazing dancing and jumping abilities.

Greece, Portugal, Italy, and Spain—the gifts, the memories, the experiences, the learnings, the wisdom just kept pouring in.

Adding all these experiences to the workshop leadership skills I developed and the people skills I learned, as well as witnessing people waking up to who they are, has been deeply etched in my being. Years of service now formed a foundation on which I could stand. I saw this existing foundation as a starting point for me to continue the reinvention of me for the next chapter of my life.

A Gem of Grief's Wisdom

Teachers are always there; they just seem to show up when the student is ready! My earnest desire and commitment to help others was somehow seen by all these rather crazy shamanic teachers. They saw something in me and poured their teachings into me in oh such a wild and generous way! Turning toward the death of my workshop career, I stumbled into all these gifts that I could now build upon.

Chapter Nine
Me a Cremationist?
Stepping into the Ring with Death

> *Live as if you were to die tomorrow. Learn as if you were to live forever.*

— Mahatma Gandhi

About a year after my rather unceremonious departure from WarriorSage, I saw an employment ad in the local newspaper. Vancouver Crematorium was looking for a cremationist. Yep, I was attracted to the job immediately!

I remembered my time in Varanasi, India, spending days on the banks of the Ganga River and witnessing firsthand the beauty of cremation. How could I take that memory, that energy, that ritual, that community approach and apply here in North America, or more accurately at the Vancouver-based crematorium looking for a cremationist?

I applied, got an interview, and was offered the job! A cremationist, I now was, and for two years, I poured myself into being just that—a compassionate cremationist. I learned a lot about the end of life and how our North American culture was now handling death. It was a new and exciting world I had just stepped into, and an early baby step on my path toward growing into an end-of-life coach, though I didn't know it at the time.

As I grew into my role as head cremationist, I recognized how much I valued the ritual, the ceremony of cremation, and how I loved to serve those grieving. I also began to realize that I didn't at all like the corporatized funeral business I was now a part of. It was such a curious time, trying to balance the corporate demands for profit and efficiency with my deeply held sense of service for those grieving. I was convinced that both were possible, yet my lived experience was suggesting the contrary.

I remember asking lots of questions of the funeral directors who worked at the crematorium. I remember many beautiful moments I experienced at witness cremations. The memories of the grievers and the answers from the funeral directors? Yep, they were at odds. The grieving families truly appreciate the ritual of cremation and the chance to say one last goodbye, while the business of the funeral home often results in unnecessary spending, such as on expensive caskets.

I recall a time right after a cremation when we had a large gathering in the witness hall adjacent to the crematorium. I was walking past the open doorway and noticed a tiny young child looking lost and overlooked by the many adults in the room. I quietly entered the hall, knelt in front of her, and asked why she looked so concerned. Her response was so precious. "That was my baba in that box, and I'm worried if she'll be okay," she said in a quiet whisper.

My response was simple. "How loving of you. I'm the man in charge of taking care of your baba, and you know what, I'll take extra special care of her just for you."

"You'll take great care of Baba just for me?" she questioned further.

I responded very simply, "Yes, I will!"

She smiled and then skipped off happily to find her folks.

At other times, I would have these bumpy conversations with the funeral team when I would ask why we would sell an expensive casket to a family that I would burn to ashes mere days after the funeral. The responses would invariably lead straight to our bottom line and the need to meet our sales targets.

I recall a time toward the end of my work as a cremationist when a father and mother came to the crematorium. Their nineteen-year-old son had just died of cancer, and they were at the crematorium to witness the cremation of their boy. At the time, my boys were the same age, and I felt a lot of compassion for Mom and Dad. As they walk into the cremation room area, a very industrial setting, I greeted them as kindly and compassionately as I could.

I asked them if they were ready for me to bring their son, lying in his casket, into the room in order that we begin the cremation process. Mom said in a quiet and shaky voice, "Yes, please." As I rolled him in on the fork-lift, they both began to cry. So, I slowed things down for them in order that they would have a chance to catch their breath and perhaps have one last goodbye. I was moved to ask, "Do you both need a little hug before we go any further?" The answer was a resounding yes, so we parents hugged.

I then asked if they would like one last look at their child before he was moved into the furnace for his cremation. They said yes, so I opened the casket, and the parents had one final goodbye with their boy. The three of us pushed the casket into the furnace. I had Mom push the button to close the furnace door, and I had Dad push the button to turn the furnace on. Their participation was an important part of their grief process.

They left slowly, thankful they had the opportunity for this final, dignified, and private farewell.

Interestingly, a few days later, I happened to be passing through the reception area at the exact time when they both came by to pick up their son's cremated remains. The clerk had placed the plastic urn on the countertop and was pushing a VISA card form toward them for a signature—in an open public space! I couldn't stand the lack of compassion for the parents and quickly stepped in and asked them to meet me in the private meeting room adjacent to the reception desk. I had the clerk get me a purple satin tote bag, and I placed the urn in the bag, grabbed the VISA form, and headed into the privacy of the meeting room. All the while, the site manager was watching the goings on.

As if holding a newborn baby, I carefully passed the beautifully bagged urn to Mom and Dad and stood with them quietly for a few minutes as the reality of their son's death sunk a little further into their hearts. Once the emotions settled, I asked for one of them to sign the VISA form, and our business was complete.

On their way out through reception, the couple asked for one final hug, to which I responded with a "Yes, of course."

Two years after I began my career as a cremationist, I was called into the site manager's office; she was joined by a human resource type. There was an envelope on the table with my name on it. I was being terminated. I guess I just didn't fit into the corporate mold they had designed for me. I wasn't the least bit surprised, and at the same time, I was sad to leave the position I loved serving in.

Another ending or non-death loss for certain, and at the same time, a doorway into yet another iteration of me. My reinvention process continued in all its magical glory.

A Gem of Grief's Wisdom

More of a question: Can compassion and enterprise not coexist?

Chapter Ten
Another Wakeup Call
Peter's Death and the Gift He Left Behind

It's the unbridled passion and the fearlessness to just go into something with reckless abandon that allows you to create something from nothing. That allows you to innovate. That allows you to take things to the extreme.

— Paul Heyman

My dear brother, Peter, had been fighting cancer for years now, and though he had some small victories along the six-and-a-half-year journey, cancer was winning the day, and the end of Peter's life was looming ever closer.

It was May 2015, and Peter was flying into Vancouver to have a treatment of targeted chemo therapy followed by a stem cell transplant process, one final medical procedure to see if his life could be saved. Though the odds were slim, it was Peter's choice, and boy, he sure wanted to live.

I was at the Vancouver International Airport, waiting for Peter to disembark from his flight from the Yukon. He and I and the rest of my family would be spending several weeks together, just in case this turned out to be Peter's swan song. Mom was there, as were sisters Sue and Carrie, and of course, Peter's wife, April, and Sonora, my wife, and extended family. We would all join in the celebrations at our Maple Ridge home.

Watching for him to come down the escalator toward the baggage claim area, I saw an old man stepping onto the moving staircase. It was Peter! I was shocked by how old, pale, tiny, and frail he looked. He was a hollow shell of his former vibrant, robust self. We hugged hello, picked up his luggage, and hopped into the car and headed home. We had the better part of a week to just hang out together as a family, to visit, to tell stories, and yes, of course, to play some cribbage—a family tradition whenever we gathered. Despite Peter's frail health and partly because of it, we had a blast!

Too soon, it seemed, we were packing Peter's stuff up to move him to the fifteenth floor at the Vancouver General Hospital. The final shot at saving Peter's life was about to begin. It was the medical system on overdrive—that was the first thing I notice as I walked into Peter's room at VGH. Machines, equipment, staff, and doctors all focused on the process of helping Peter. Oddly, it seemed not so much focused on Peter himself.

Mom and April were in the hospital room keeping him company as machines whirred, lights blinked, and staff attended to all manner of equipment, all somehow plugged into Peter's body through ports in his chest and IVs in his arms. It all seemed so unreal and oh so serious at the same time. There was this heavy feel to the room, somber and dark, as if death were lurking in the corner just out of sight.

I couldn't help myself; my irreverent side was screaming to be heard. So, I said in a comedic tone, "Good morning, Chemosabe, how are you doing today?" The room took an inhale and held its breath, waiting for some kind of acknowledgement. Mother dear was shocked, yet Peter, in his customary way, smiled and said, "Tonto pretty shit but glad to see you!" Peter's permission given, there was a chorus of giggles and some laughs at the humour he and I often shared in our lives. This was the right medicine for everyone. We all needed a good laugh. It was serious stuff we were all witnessing, yet there needed to be room to breathe too. I was happy to provide the comic relief!

The month Peter spent at VGH, going through this last-ditch attempt to rid his body of cancer, was extremely tough on all levels. His body took a huge beating. It was tough on all of us mentally and emotionally. Spiritually, we were all looking for a clear resolution one way or the other. It had been a long six years, and we were eager for an answer and some much-needed relief.

Treatment finished, and Peter and April returned home to Creston, BC, to rest, recover, and wait for the call. Months later, Peter got the call they had long been awaiting. It wasn't good news, and in his own words, Peter said, "The medical system just kicked me to the curb, Stephen."

Peter's death was now clearly on the near-term horizon.

My sister Carrie and I arrived in Creston, BC, a couple of weeks before Peter's death. We wanted to both support April in giving end-of-life care to Peter and also to be there for Peter in his final days. And that's exactly what we did!

Peter's health care and pain management needs demanded that he be moved from the family home to the Butterfly Room (the hospice room) in the Creston General Hospital. So, we all set about making it as much like home as possible. We brought in his own blankets, some memorabilia, some books, and a few hockey jerseys. We hung a sign on the door that said, "Knock before entering please." After all, this was to be where Peter would take his final breath, and we intended that it be as comfortable and homelike as possible for him.

We spent each day by Peter's side. We had great chats, enjoyed common memories, and often gave Peter gentle touch and massage to help ease the pain his body was experiencing. As the days passed, we all noticed his energy began to wane. We decided it was important to have only two or three of us with Peter at a time to preserve his limited life energy. So, we scheduled visits to match his energy's capacity.

Peter was actively dying.

He began to refuse food and drink.

His body became more and more still.

He was getting ready to take his last breath sometime much sooner than later.

With Peter's death so close at hand, April and I decided it was time to head to the funeral home, and GF Oliver's was just two blocks from the Creston General Hospital, so off we went. We were clear on what Peter wanted, and that was a basic cremation, no frills, plain and simple.

Arrangements were made for what the funeral director called a basic cremation. A cardboard casket, a plastic temporary urn, and no ceremony. Once Peter's death was pronounced, April was to call the funeral home and they would come and pick Peter up and, with her permission, proceed with the cremation. It felt odd and kind of otherworldly to be making arrangements for my dear younger brother's cremation. Even though we were well prepared and knew what we wanted, it just seemed a little unreal.

Death-bed regrets were next on the list, and two days before he died, Peter and I were alone in the hospice room. Everyone else was out for a much-needed break and a bite to eat. I had a burning desire to ask him if he had any life regrets. So, I took a deep breath and asked him just that. He had two regrets to share.

First, he spoke about how shitty he felt because of all the chemo and radiation he had poured into his body in order to live. He felt he should have treated his body with more respect and love. I totally understood Peter and simply said, "Thanks."

His second regret was much more difficult for him to speak out loud. It was also heartbreaking for me to hear. "Stephen, I'm sixty-one years old, and I never fully jumped in and lived my life. I always held back by 12 per cent. I never really let myself loose to just live full on." We both started to cry at the sadness of it all. I hopped up on his bed, and we simply held each other and cried. There was nothing else to do, and clearly nothing to say. Two brothers weeping deeply over a life not fully lived.

Peter was clear that he wanted only his wife and his sister Carrie by his side when he was dying. It was his wish for sure, and we all were on board with Pete's end-of-life wishes; after all, we were there to serve him in his dying days and ways.

The day of his death had arrived, and it was time for me to say goodbye. It was a Thursday, interestingly the same day of the week my dear sister Jody died. He was fading quickly, and it was clear to both the hospice staff and to us that today was his death day. It was around noon, and he and I had one last goodbye. "See you next time, dear brother" were my final words to Peter. I kissed him on his forehead and turned to leave.

I took one last look at him as I left the room and was immediately struck by Shakespeare's words: "Parting is such sweet sorrow." The sweetness was the spiritual side. We actually knew each other, and his suffering was about to end. The sorrow was the human side of the coin. We would never hug again; our human life together was soon to be over, and that was damn sad.

I hopped into my car and headed west back toward Vancouver. I had just pulled into my driveway when my cell phone buzzed. A text had just arrived. It was from April, Peter's amazing wife. Interestingly, it was around 9:00 p.m.—the same time I'd received the call from Roy about Jody's death.

"He's gone."

I cried deeply, lit a candle, and placed a picture of Peter on my altar.

A year later in Whitehorse, Yukon, we held Peter's celebration of life, and a celebration it was! We had decided shortly after his death that we all wanted to let the dust settle after his long journey with cancer, and it was true that we all needed a rest, especially emotionally. So, we set a time a year away and began to slowly set the plans in place for Peter's celebration.

Family and friends filled the hall we had rented, and there was such a buzz in the air, you could feel the love we all shared for him. It was a glorious day filled with Peter stories, photos, notes, and love letters. We laughed and cried, we giggled and chatted, we all honoured the thing we had in common—my dear brother, Peter!

We placed a large scrapbook on a table with a photograph of Peter and the simple instruction: Write Peter a love note, a poem, or a story you remember him by. There was a supply of pens and crayons handy and a chair to sit on while reflecting back on sweet Peter. It was the favourite spot of most every-

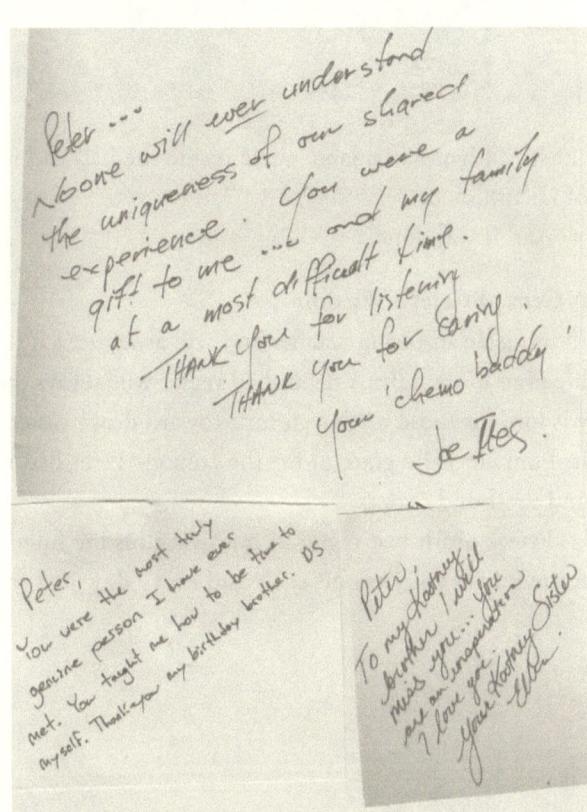

one gathered there. The result was a beautiful outpouring of people's love for Peter, and it was a great keepsake for April.

Mom held court close by and chatted with all those who came to visit. It was bittersweet for her to hear how much people loved her son and how much they missed him. April was close by too, as were Carrie and Sue.

It was time to say goodbye to Peter, so April picked up the

urn that held his ashes and we all walked out to the riverside to witness his release into the Yukon River. April held him close to her heart, and when she was ready, she lovingly sprinkled him into the beautiful flowing waters of the Yukon River that would take Peter well into nature's womb.

We gathered in a large circle inside the hall and toasted Peter with a shot of Glenfiddich.

And it was done.

A Gem of Grief's Wisdom

Death is an inspiring teacher and will always teach those present how to live life even more fully. A death-bed regret will always morph into a piece of life wisdom for those willing to turn toward death instead of turning away from it. I am eternally grateful for the courage Peter had to share such a personal and profound regret.

Peter's death-bed regret of not living his life fully turned into a life lesson for me: **Live your ass off each and every day, just in case.** Thanks, Peter!

Chapter Eleven
Another Reminder—Dear Mom's Passing
Everything Is Impermanent

> *Rituals give grief a place to go …*
>
> — Sabina Galay

The final years of Mom's life had been spent living with her daughter Carrie, who was joined by sister Sue for the final year, as Mom's care demands had increased significantly. It was a busy and happy family home, the place where Mom wanted to die.

As a family we had gotten much better at these end-of-life things. Jody's, Dad's, and Peter's dying and death had taught us lots; we learned over the years how to prepare for the unavoidable end of life. So, we were well prepared for Mom's eventual death.

- ✓ will done
- ✓ care directives done
- ✓ power of attorney done
- ✓ executor appointed
- ✓ expected letter of death in the home signed by the doctor
- ✓ funeral plans made and paid for
- ✓ final visits planned

Carrie and I spoke often, and in early July, it seemed like it was time for me to head east to Waterloo, Ontario, and say my final goodbyes to dear mother Marge, the person with whom I had my longest-lasting relationship—seventy-three years! Booked the flight, hopped on a plane, and was soon in the family home with Mom, Sue, and Carrie—the final four together again. It was weird knowing we would soon be three.

Mom was good. She was just old and nearing the end of her amazing life of almost a century! Her body was tired, as was her mind. It was obvious she was nearing the end; she knew it and spoke of it, and we all included her end-of-life chats as a part of our now daily life. We worked with her on preparing to go as opposed to the more common approach of denying death and urging her to focus on the positives and to struggle to live on. Carrie, a personal services worker, was awesome and knew exactly what to do to support Mom physically and mentally, and emotionally too.

Sue was a great support, and between the two sisters and the support of community health care nurses, Marge was well taken care of. The two daughters took great self-care! They made sure to schedule in off time, shopping time, and coffee breaks on a regular daily basis. No caregiver burnout here!

So, we all settled into a nice family visit, and I spent lots of time with dear mom. It was both sweet and sad to see her. Sweet because she's my mom, yet sad to see her so close to the end of her life, struggling to eat, drink, and find her words. Everything physical was a challenge for Mom, from getting in and out of her recliner, to getting to the bathroom. Getting in and out of bed was also a big challenge. About the only thing that wasn't a challenge for the "old girl" was sleeping.

Over the days we were together, we told lots of family stories and remembered out loud what it was like growing up, always within earshot of Mom. There was one particular conversation we all had that I will always remember. I wanted Mom to know that she would live on through her children, so I told her some stories about all her children and linked it to Mom's desire to always help people out.

I reminded Mom of Peter's work with the First Nations bands in the Yukon and then linked it to her. "Guess where Pete got his desire to help others from, Mom?" I asked. Mom smiled demurely, and I said, "From you, Mother dear!

"Mom, look at Susie. She spent years in Nunavut teaching and supporting the Inuit peoples. She got her love of supporting others from you, Mom. See, two for two so far." I smiled.

"And then there's Carrie, who's a personal services worker for seniors," I continued. "See, Mom, you're alive in Susie and Carrie! And if that's not enough evidence, look at your eldest child: me." I sat still for a minute or two to let it all sink in. Mom was quiet and smiling at the same time.

"See, Mom, you'll live on through your kids. Your loving legacy is in good hands. So, when it's time for you to go, it's okay. We have you living in our hearts." Mom smiled with tears running down her cheeks. We held hands for a while and just sat together as a family basking in the afterglow of our love for each other.

The rest of the visit was fun, with outings here and there, great chats, and fun meals. It all went by way too fast, and my final day of visiting was upon us. I leaned over to kiss Mom goodbye and said to her, "See you next time."

Mom smiled, winked, and returned with "This life or next life, Stevie?"

And that was it.

A month later, on August 25, 2022, at 4:51 a.m. EDT, I received a text from dear sister Carrie: "Mom has just died." I cried and lit a candle on my altar for her. Her picture now joins Jody's, Peter's, Dad's, and brother-in-law Ronnie's photos.

The next Saturday, the west coast Garrett family gathered at our place and joined the east coasters for Mom's ceremony on, of all things, Zoom. The funeral home had a great setup that allowed family and friends not living in the area to join the celebration. It was actually lovely to be there in real time with all my family and watch and listen to the goings on—one of the benefits of the modern digital age. It was interesting to notice who was there. It was mostly offspring: kids, grandkids, and great-grandkids. Mom had outlived all of her friends and siblings. It was way different than Dad's funeral, as he had died relatively young, at seventy-nine, so he had friends and family who survived him there to say goodbye. All the same, it was a sweet ceremony, and I'm so glad to have been there virtually.

We were once seven; now we are three: Susie, Carrie, and me.

A Gem of Grief's Wisdom
When it comes to the end of life, don't wait to say and share what's in your heart. Don't wait for spring, as it turns into regret. Just in case, speak your heart's words today!

Section Three

Becoming Grief's Walking Stick:
My Personal Journey from Sorrow to Service Matures

Chapter Twelve
Going All In
Waking Up to My Calling

*Discovering your purpose is the most significant thing you will
do in your life, and you, your loved ones, and the world will
be better off because you went on this journey.*

— Mastin Kipp

Well, what to do now?
It seemed I wasn't a great fit with corporations or organizations, so I
thought I'd set out on my own. Recently inspired by my dear brother Peter's
death-bed regret, I chose to step into the role of an end-of-life coach. My
new business venture would be coaching individuals and families through
the tangled knots of dying, death, and grief. My wife, Sonora, wondered out
loud if I'd be able to make a living at it. Personally, I had no doubt—or at
least, so I thought.

Over the years, I had developed a solid personal relationship with God,
or The Divine, or The One, or The Creator, or whatever name you choose to
give your own higher power. I refer to Her lovingly as Grandmother. It was
kind of Her idea for me to work in the field of dying, death, and grief. And,
I mean, who am I to suggest She doesn't know what She's doing! So, I agreed
and off I went on this new adventure to be an end-of-life coach and death
educator. It felt very much like I had been called to this sacred work.

I created a couple of websites, aliveindeath.ca and wecandiebetter.com, and I
began to market myself to the world as an end-of-life coach and educator. Emails
to care homes and hospices. Letters to nursing associations and colleges. Calls to

friends and colleagues in the healing industry. Hmmm, no matter what energy I put in, it felt like a slow-go, and I wasn't making much headway. I persevered, though, and just kept at it despite the lack of initial results.

It was a bumpy nine years, with lots of downs and not too many ups. I remember about two or three years into my "job" as an end-of-life coach and trainer, it wasn't going too well at all. I had sent out hundreds of flyers, hundreds of emails, and done tons of pro-bono conferences and workshops. It was going slowly, and on the financial side, I was running out of patience. I remember one day calling Grandma (my term of endearment for God) to my office to give Her a piece of my mind. I was so pissed off at the way things were going and how slowly things were moving.

I ranted and raged for a while, a long while at that. Yet Grandmother was patient with me, and when I was through, She asked, "Stephen, honey, don't you trust me?"

Well, this is God asking, and She already knew the answer. I needed to own it myself, so I simply said, "No, I don't."

Expecting a scolding, I braced myself. I was surprised by Grandmother's next question: "Well, would you like to, honey?"

"Well, of course, I would, Grandma," I replied immediately.

"Then Stephen, just make the choice to trust Me."

I sat in stunned silence for what seemed like hours. I was thinking to myself, *All I have to do is choose to trust God?* Yet, for some reason, I struggled to make that choice. Finally, I broke through and made that simple yet oddly challenging choice. All Grandma said was "Well done, honey. See you soon." And off She went.

I lay on the floor of my home office and cried for an hour or two. Looking back, I do believe they were tears of joy. Interestingly, I remember feeling no longer alone. It was as if my choice to trust Grandma had welcomed Her fully into my life. Things started to go markedly better for me.

Though my first attempt in the end-of-life world as a cremationist was a bust, I was looking for another way in, and finally in early 2017, I stepped into the role as the executive director of the Memorial Society of BC, a position that lasted until September 2020, when the COVID-19 pandemic forced some tough financial decisions for the society, and my voluntary departure was one of them.

I had begun teaching with Rhodes Wellness College in 2016 and was able to continue in my grief and loss work until I landed another position with Campbell River Hospice Society as their remote grief and loss counsellor, a position I held until May 2022, when I resigned for personal reasons. I needed a break and to refocus on what my heart now wanted to do. I had done a lot of frontline work over the years and now found myself wanting to teach and mentor more as opposed to doing the emotionally demanding work as a counsellor.

I continued my work with Rhodes Wellness College as a facilitator and trainer and began to co-create with them the Professional End-of-Life Facilitator Program. Everything was magically falling into place again. This time, though, it felt like I had my legs underneath me, and the movement was now almost always in the forward direction. I was teaching, coaching, and mentoring, feeling much more like Grief's Walking Stick. I was feeling as if I had found my personal seat in life.

A Gem of Grief's Wisdom
Trust is a very big word! Ease to say it, just rolls off the tongue, and at the same time, it's really hard to truly embrace. Persistence, though challenging, pays off!

Chapter Thirteen
In the End …
The Elder Emerges

> *Teachings come from everywhere when you open yourself to them. That's the trick of it, really. Open yourself to everything, and everything opens itself to you.*

— Richard Wagamese

It was the summer of 2022, and I'd taken my Bodhisattva vows with Mingyur Rinpoche, a Tibetan Buddhist monk and teacher I had met a year earlier. A bodhisattva takes a vow to step into the suffering in the world in order to help alleviate it. I didn't realize what was going on underneath all the learning, studying, and practising I was doing, yet now looking back, I see that I was stepping forward into my elderhood.

To help me along my path, dear Mom was nearing the end of her life. She had turned ninety-four and was "ready to go," in her words. As I mentioned in chapter eleven, she was living at home with sister Carrie and her husband, Charles; sister Sue had joined in to support her care. They were all accompanied by Kali the cat and Angel the dog, the love brigade. Dear mom was in an environment of great loving care.

Mom's death on August 25, 2022, was the next natural stepping stone along my path. We were once a family of seven, and now all of a sudden (it seemed) we are down to just three. I once was seven, and I am now seventy-four. Wow, that's a whole lot of life and death! Perhaps now, it's time to explore this life I've lived for the gems of wisdom I know I have picked up along the way.

I am now the eldest Garrett in my lineage. I carry the Garrett family mantel, so to speak. There is no one above me in my family to whom I can go to for advice or wisdom. I am it! Hmmm ... a not so gentle nudge into my elderhood, it seems. So, it appears on many levels, I am indeed stepping into elderhood and, interestingly, not begrudgingly. It is not "damn, I'm getting older." For me, it feels more like "Yes, I am so excited to see what is yet to come."

All my work on dying, death, and grief also seems to have an effect on my own maturing. Being rested in my own impermanent nature, my own death, and my aging has become just another step along the path of my life, one that I welcome as opposed to one that I turn away from, because it seems death is just around the corner.

The elder in me is emerging, and I am stepping more fully each day into that place of service, that time of planting seeds of wisdom in the youngers. A time of personal reflection and discovery. It is a sacred and important time indeed, a time that is much needed as we continue to grow and evolve along life's spiritual path.

From my perspective, there's a huge difference between a senior and an elder, and it's worth noting. The senior perspective is more aligned with ageism, the turn of a calendar page or the change of a number. It seems that seniors take a different tact with aging than do elders. It seems as if seniors turn away from dying and death, hoping beyond hope to avoid it entirely or pass away in their sleep.

An elder, though, seems to embrace their entire life, including aging, retirement, and death. Retirement from the elders' perspective means changing what they do with the time they have left; you might say reinventing themselves. It usually means being of service to others.

Here is a table that clearly shows the differences I see between a senior and an elder.

The Issue	The Senior	The Elder
Relationship	Becomes more isolated	Becomes more connected
Worldview	The end is near	A new beginning is at hand
Life Energy	Contracting and resentful	Expanding and content

View of Death	Denial and resignation	Acceptance and possibility
Approach to Life	Unavoidable losses	Chooses opportunity
Life Focus	Indifference	Making a difference

It's a bit of a bumpy road, this retirement thing, and we tend to move through four distinct stages or phases before we end up in either the narrow world of a senior or the space of opportunities afforded by the world of the elder.

The first phase is much like the honeymoon phases of a relationship, like the early days of summer vacation. Freedom, everything seems new and fresh. No restraints, and we are sort of untethered. It's fun for a while, usually a year or two at most, and then reality sets in and we fall into stage two.

The second stage features a recognition of all we have lost as we step from the world of work to the world of retirement. It can be a challenging time indeed, as the grief builds up given all the non-death losses retirees have experienced. It can be easy to get stuck in the funk of stage two.

The next and third phase is a time of exploration, where we have stepped out of the often gloomy second stage and have now chosen to check out some possibilities, some areas of interest we could dive into. Things we could do that bring us a sense of fulfillment. We can stumble in this stage if we don't have initial success in finding something new to do, and fall back into the gloomy second stage. However, if we do find something that gets our juices flowing, stage four awaits.

The final stage is a time of joy and satisfaction, as we have discovered what it is we want to do and we have begun doing it. It usually involves service to others.

A Gem of Grief's Wisdom
There's a difference between a senior and an elder. The senior is recognized mostly by the tick of a clock or the turning of a page on a calendar. The elder is recognized mostly by the presence of spirit's wisdom within them and their willingness to share it.

Chapter Fourteen
Grief's Walking Stick I Am
Simply Being Me—A Sigh of Relief

> *Even though our time in this life is temporary, if we live well*
> *enough, our legacy will last forever.*

— Idowu Koyenikan

O ne of the things I have learned over the many years of my life is a little gem of wisdom that is oh so very easy to miss:

Simply being my authentic self IS enough!!!

Yep, you read it correctly! Being my authentic self is enough. I don't have to be an anything or an everything, or a nothing. I don't have to be a some-body or a nobody. Simply being me, myself, is—without a doubt—enough. And being me unapologetically is the icing on the cake.

In the world of dying, death, grief, and loss, this means that me, my presence, is enough. Simply being with those who have suffered the loss of a loved one as the human I am, with the dying, death, and grief wisdom I carry, is enough to be helpful. Sharing my own stories and wisdom with the bereaved does, in fact, help them. Being a human being with the one dying is truly supportive.

What this all means is that you, too, are enough. The rub is that we're all trained throughout our lives to be a somebody or a something in order to be of value to others. So, we set out to become a something or a someone almost always at the cost of giving up or giving away who we truly are at our core.

That being said, death demands authenticity!

Our masked self, our protected self, just won't do. When death comes knocking on the door of a loved one, or on our own door, it demands that we, the one we truly are, show up. Dying and ultimately death are real-life opportunities to awaken to the magnificence we have generally kept hidden our entire lives. As I have continued to walk more consciously into my role as a death guide, coach, doula, or educator—or perhaps even death shaman—I have been humbled to learn that I am enough. Just me is exactly what dying and death require, no more and no less. Just the authentic good heart I've always been.

I remember, years ago, a man who epitomized this walking stick philosophy. I was living on the Sunshine Coast of British Columbia, working in Sechelt. My office was nearby Pebble Beach, and within sight was a park bench overlooking the ocean. Often a fellow sat on that bench, seemingly just staring out over the ocean view. I noticed him nearly every day just sitting there, as if he had nothing better to do. I must admit that I was a little critical of him. *What a waste of a life*, I thought to myself.

Then one day a young man walking along the path stopped in front of this fellow. The old guy motioned for him to sit down. The young man did. I noticed an intense conversation going on, and at one point, the old fella threw his arm around the young man. The conversation came to an end, they had a brief hug, and the young man waved and walked off, a little happier than he was before the chat.

Days later, another similar scene with a woman in her midlife played out. And then a young child. And then an older man. It seemed as if this fellow was of some sort of support for all these people. It then dawned on me that the park bench was his office, and the folks who stopped by were his clients. He would simply sit in his office patiently until a client needed him.

I remember heading over to see him one afternoon. I decided to be straight with him and told him this story. At the end of our chat, he offered me a hug and said, "Hope it helped." He smiled, I waved, and off I went.

Hmmm, my first experience with the notion of Grief's Walking Stick. This is where my walking stick philosophy began, yet it didn't bloom fully for several decades. The seed had been planted, but I didn't yet realize it.

A Gem of Grief's Wisdom
An undisturbed heart full of compassion is the most comfortable couch in which to rest, heal, and share your grief.

Grief's Walking Stick Tool Box
A Manual for Your Walk with Death and Grief

Tool Number One
The Seven Languages of Sorrow
How Grief Can Be Expressed

Tool Number Two
The All Ready to Go Binder
Getting Your End-of-Life Paperwork Together

Tool Number Three
Different Types of Loss
And the Grief That Goes with Them

Tool Number Four
Creating a Ritual for My Family
Tailor-Made Celebrations

Tool Number Five
Before I Go Template
Gems of Wisdom to Share with Others

Tool Number Six
The Grief Tree
A Place for Community to Gather

Tool Number One
The Seven Languages of Sorrow
How Grief Can Be Expressed

I had long thought that love has no opposite, yet over the past few years, I've realized that it may not have an opposite, but it certainly has a twin! Love and grief work as a unique team that truly supports our growth and evolution as spiritual beings living this beautifully raw human life.

However, a note of caution:

Too much love and we can turn into an artificial sweetie.
Too much grief and we can turn into a sour and bitter person.

The practice, I have found, is to let myself be affected by both the love and the grief, as both teach me important lessons about living in the here and now. The languages of love and the languages of grief are decidedly unique in and of themselves and in how they get expressed by each different, unique individual.

The big Love and the individual love, along with the big Grief and the personal grief, will, when we open to them, show us the importance of compassion, kindness, gratitude, authenticity, and acceptance. The inseparable pair of Love and Grief can help us grow from being centred on self to being focused on serving others.

A note of caution—it takes both Love and Grief to grow!

Linked to the thought of love and grief being twins, I recall reading a book about love languages and found myself wondering about grief languages. Does grief have different voices, and if so, what are the languages of grief? I have discovered many forms of grief's expression over my years of work with dying, death, and loss. Here is a list of seven of the primary ones:

1. Verbal Expression

Interpersonal communication, talk therapy, support groups

2. Written Expression

Letters, poetry, lyrics, prose, texts, emails

3. Emotional Expression

Drumming or music, expression of feelings, making noises

4. Physical Expression

Dance or body movement, hiking, walking, swimming, throwing

5. Spiritual Expression

Ritual, prayer, meditation, or ceremony

6. Artistic Expression

Painting, weaving, carving, sculpting, gardening

7. Avoidant Expression

No direct communication, tucked away, filed, handled

No one way is superior to another, and very often individuals rely on two or three of the languages to communicate fully to others the grief they're experiencing. There will be a primary or preferred first choice, often backed up by one or two other languages.

Typically, in North America, we expect grief to be delivered in two primary forms: verbal and emotional, which limits and disenfranchises people with different grief languages. Because of our culture's view of how grief is to be expressed, and its denial of grief in general, we tend to miss the other unique forms of expression. As a result, we leave some folks feeling unseen and unheard in their grief. Our death- and grief-denying culture makes it difficult for many of us to learn how to express our grief and how many ways that expression can be demonstrated.

Let's begin our exploration of the Seven Languages of Sorrow. I have given each language a nickname for easy reference and also to make the language more colourfully human.

1. Verbal Expression—The Talker

Interpersonal communication, talk therapy, and support groups

The Talker typically prefers to use words and language to express themselves. Secondarily, they may use the written word, perhaps with a touch of emotions. Being most comfortable intellectually, it is rare, though not impossible, to find ***The Talker*** dabbling in the arts or in movement. Explore with ***The Talker*** the other five grief languages to discover with them what their secondary and tertiary preferences are.

In order to support someone whose preference is ***The Talker***, we need to understand that using words is their natural way to express themselves. By talking with them, we actually help them move forward with their grief, even though it may not feel like it to us. Sometimes a good balance for ***The Talker*** is to use the written word and to devote some time to putting their thoughts down on paper. In taking this slightly different approach and still using words, ***The Talker***, while in this more reflective space, may bump into some emotions.

Another approach is to take ***The Talker*** for a walk and do a walk and talk session. The action of moving the body physically out in nature provides a different talking space than perhaps ***The Talker*** is accustomed to. The addition of movement and nature often results in more emotional connection, which supports the spoken word.

It's important to remember not to force *The Talker* to use grief languages that are foreign to them, as this type of pressure usually results in them shutting down and feeling judged that their talking is somehow not good enough or lacking.

A Client Story

His wife of twenty-five years died in his arms, and instantly, his life was changed forever. As I got to know him, I realized that his natural language of grief was simply to talk. He wasn't much for emotions and for sure wasn't a writer. He was a talker, though.

So, we talked together through his grief, and week by week, he began to get back into his life. He told me stories of him and his wife and adventures they'd shared. He told me that he was staying in his travel trailer, as he couldn't face being in the family home without her. He told me stories of visiting her gravesite and of his step-children who visited the site with him from time to time.

He told me story after story, and as he did, he came to realize that though sad, he could go on without her. Her told me of his moving back into the family home and how he chose to sleep in the guest bedroom. He told me stories of preparing meals with a little extra for his dear deceased wife.

I asked him once if he would like to write her a love letter, a goodbye letter, and his initial answer was clear and direct: "No." So, we continued to talk it out session by session. He ultimately told me he would write the love letter when he was feeling more stable and able. He also told me when our sessions were done.

A pure *Talker* he was, and all I needed to do was simply be patient and listen to him, providing a little direction and guidance when necessary.

2. Written Expression—The Writer

Letters, poetry, lyrics, prose, texts, social media posts, and emails

The Writer is similar in many ways to the talker and may be more introverted than their more talkative counterpart. They find comfort in the written word and, in a real way, feel secure being behind the words. ***The Writer*** may have many written outlets for their words that can include such things as emails, texts, and social media posts, to name but a few. Poetry, letters, and prose are also common for the older writers who may not be so familiar with things digital.

As with the talker, ***The Writer*** is at home putting pen to paper. Finding ways to help them express their grief in various written forms will truly support them in moving forward in their grief process.

The Writer might have, as additional languages, The Talker, or perhaps The Artist, and maybe a touch of The Sensitive One, so explore with them the other five grief languages to discover their secondary and tertiary preferences.

To support ***The Writer***, we can offer them a selection of written formats to use. One I find most helpful is letter writing to the deceased loved one. Often when the writing is made personal by addressing the note or letter to the person by name, some emotions linked to the writing come up. It's often the privacy of letter writing coupled with the intimacy of writing to someone that may help *The Writer* get in touch with their emotions.

In some cases, you might consider note writing in a grief session with a person whose preference is to write. They may be feeling so overwhelmed and numbed by the death they experienced that even a little speaking is too difficult for them in the moment. Using a pad of paper and writing notes back and forth may provide the safety needed by *The Writer* in that moment. As with the other grief languages, remember not to force a foreign language on *The Writer*, as the result can often be writer's block.

A Client Story or Two

A young teenage client of mine wasn't particularly fond of talking, especially face-to-face. They found it way more comfortable to text. So, text we did. We used their preferred method, *The Writer*, and took it a natural step further. They would text a question or comment to me, and I would text a response back to them. Every so often, we'd have a short chat just to say hello and catch-up mouth-to-ear instead of eye-to-eye.

Text-based healing sessions were a little odd for me, yet they sure worked for them, so we continued for several months until one day I received a call from them: "Thanks so much for doing it my way. Our texting really helped me get through the death of my friend."

Client Two

A woman client of mine had just experienced the death of her brother, and she was a little numb and deeply sad. They were close as brother and sister, yet they didn't talk much. She had lots to say to him in hindsight and many kind words for how he was always there for her. As we continued our sessions together, letter writing and poetry came up as options, and she jumped all over them both.

She wrote a love letter and then a poem to him, and in a session one day, she read them both to me. Tears of joy and sadness rolled down her cheeks as she recognized just how much he meant to her. The letter and poem writing helped her move forward in her love/grief of her dear brother. She was a combination of *The Talker* and *The Writer*, and the use of both tools was instrumental in her working through her grief.

3. Emotional Expression—The Sensitive One
Drumming or music, expression of feelings, and making sounds

The Sensitive One feels deeply and is emotionally adept. They're most at home when they feel their way through life. Though their secondary languages may be art or movement, they can often become overwhelmed and almost paralyzed by the depth of emotions they feel. Working with *The Sensitive One* will require deep presence and often silence and stillness. Remember to explore with them the other five grief languages to discover their secondary and tertiary preferences.

It's best to have options when in session with *The Sensitive One*, such as pens, paint and brushes, canvases, and a book of art paper. Sometimes even musical instruments are useful. These are tools that will support their full emotional expression and allow for the fullness of their feelings.

Sometimes *The Sensitive One* is so full of rich feelings that they have a challenge just putting names to them all. Trying to name them can actually block their emotional flow. It can be better just to have them make a sound, either with their voice or with a drum or musical instrument.

Emotions and intellect are strange bedfellows and most often do not play well together. It's best to discover within *The Sensitive One* which other languages align best for them, and it is often art and movement. Again, refrain from forcing *The Sensitive One* to use languages that don't align with their deepest heart. Forcing a foreign language on them usually results in them freezing or shutting down.

A Client Story

This fine young boy was dealing with the suicide of his biological father. Though they hadn't lived together for a while, they stayed in touch weekly by telephone or Skype. My first session with him and his mom taught me lots about his preferred way of communicating. While we were chatting on a Zoom call, I noticed that he was a real doodler. His attention was more on his drawing than on our talking. So, *The Sensitive One* was showing me his second language: *The Artist*.

I encouraged his mom to go make a cup of tea, so he and I had a few minutes together. I asked him to show me what he was drawing, and he happily pulled out his sketch book and began sharing with me many of his drawings. I asked him if he would prefer to draw me his feelings instead of talking about them. He responded with a huge smile and a quiet yes. So, sketch we did, and each week for a while, he and I communicated his grief out by his drawing and my reading his drawings back to him.

All his drawing we in blacks and greys until the day he presented me with his "graduation" sketch. It was a drawing of him standing in a field with a bunch of helium balloons attached to his wrist, flying high over his head. The balloons spelled out his name in glorious bright colours! He was back and alive, and our work together was done. We both happily said goodbye for now.

4. Physical Expression—The Mover and Shaker
Dance or body movement, hiking, walking, swimming, and breath work

The Mover and Shaker, like the sensitive one, often feels deeply, and their preferred way through their grief is to move the body, to shake the emotions out. Sandy Oshiro Rosen, in her epic book *Bare: The Misplaced Art of*

Grieving and Dancing, writes of the misplaced art of grieving and dancing. She knows full well that dance and movement for many people is their way of grieving, as they let the body do the talking.

The Mover and Shaker may also hike in nature or go for long walks as a way to connect with spirit and allow nature to support them by whisking away the grief they are releasing. As with the talker, often a walk and talk session out in nature can be very supportive for **The Mover and Shaker**, as the movement of the body often loosens the tongue.

Explore with **The Mover and Shaker** the other five grief languages to discover with them their secondary and tertiary preferences. Art and poetry are often a good fit, and in some cases, breathwork may be a workable tool. Using the breath to open the body often brings out both emotions and spirit. Sandy Oshiro Rosen's book is well worth the read.

A Client Story

Her husband had recently died of a drug overdose, and she was beyond herself with anger and profound sorrow. They'd had an up and down relationship due to his addiction, yet they both really loved each other and, most times, got along beautifully. He was an occasional binger, and on one binge, he simply never returned.

She was stuck in her grief process, and her anger was eating her up. As we got to know each other, it became clear that she was a **Mover and Shaker**. She was a very physical woman, and we needed to find a way to support her in using her body to express her emotions.

One day, we stumbled on a possible solution: an angry dance out in the woods near a stream or creek with a friend there as support and witness. The date was set, the angry dance was planned, and off she and her friend went. Her friend videotaped segments of the barefoot dance of anger. It was vital, alive, and very physical. She truly expressed her anger through her dancing, and she reported later the relief she felt as the anger left her body and was, in her words, absorbed by Mother Nature.

Once much of the anger was expressed, the sadness and sorrow of her loss came through with grace and ease. She simply sat and cried, allowing **The Sensitive One**, her second language, to take over.

5. Spiritual Expression—The Seeker
Ritual, prayer, meditation, or ceremony

The Seeker will naturally and sometimes spontaneously pray or fall into meditation. It is their familiar language, and so often, we can mistake prayer or meditation as an avoidance or not real grief work. Genuine prayer or meditation actually brings *The Seeker* closer to their loved one and closer to spirit at the same time, deeply supporting their more internal grief process.

The Seeker is often born "knowing" spirit, and for them, it's natural and effortless to pray or meditate to be with the Divine. It's not a practice but a way of living. There is no separation between them and spirit and others. Rituals and ceremonies are normal ways for them to express love and loss, so supporting them in the creation of rituals is extremely valuable. It's often in the planning and preparation of a ritual or a ceremony that healing takes place.

Explore with *The Seeker* the other five grief languages to discover with them their secondary and tertiary preferences, along with their spiritual preference. Again, you may find tools like art and poetry are a good fit.

In the case of *The Seeker*, the talker may actually be a good fit, as they find that talking through their prayer, meditation, or ritual experiences actually deepens their process. Also, death can bring with it an existential crisis in the form of questions like "What is the meaning of life?"

A Client Story

Her husband had died suddenly and unexpectedly, and she found herself lost in an ocean of emotions—in her words, "a tsunami of feelings." Her anchor was a newly kindled interest in her culture's spiritual wisdom. Her intentional curiosity led her to understanding the power of prayer and the importance of ritual.

Our sessions together became a planning space for the rituals she would create and then execute, always much to her relief. So, the talking we did was mostly around planning and preparation. It was in the completion of the tailor-made rituals where she expressed her many shades of sorrow.

She danced, she drummed, and she used fire for burnings and cold stream waters for cleansing, always in the presence of a friend who was both witness to her expression and supporter in life. She shared her rituals with me by video. We didn't need to talk about them, as there was no need to. Over time and after many rituals, she had found her way back home to herself, her heart, and her life.

6. Artistic Expression—The Artist
Painting, weaving, carving, sculpting, and gardening

The Artist feels at home expressing themselves through some form of art. Painting, sculpting, and carving are three such forms of artwork that work well as an outlet for grief. If you watch them closely, you'll notice that they pour themselves into their work, as if what's inside gets magically transported onto the canvas, into the pottery, or into the carving.

Explore with **The Artist** the other five grief languages to discover with them their secondary and tertiary preferences. You may find that they lean away from languages that are more intellectual, while they may lean into movement or perhaps rituals.

Two other art forms are weaving and gardening, and these expressions can be equally helpful in supporting them in getting through their grief. Planting living things in a garden is often a good counterbalance right after a death. The rhythm in weaving, the to-and-fro of the tapestry needle, can be very healing.

A Client Story or Two

I was chatting with a new client when I noticed on the wall behind them a beautiful woven wall hanging, so I asked them about it. Well, as it turned out, they had woven it themselves, and they had a studio in their home with a loom in it. The idea of the grieving weaver was born, and over the next weeks and months, a beautiful blanket was woven for her dear brother, who was very close to death. Using her primary language of sorrow, *The Artist*, she was easily able to express herself and the grief she was feeling as she dealt with the fact that her brother was dying. Words didn't do it for her, but weaving did.

Over the weeks and months that followed, she would often send me short videos of her weaving this blanket—her love for her brother made manifest—with short descriptors of what she was doing. And as the weaving and grieving continued, she began to settle more gracefully into the reality that her dear brother was very near death.

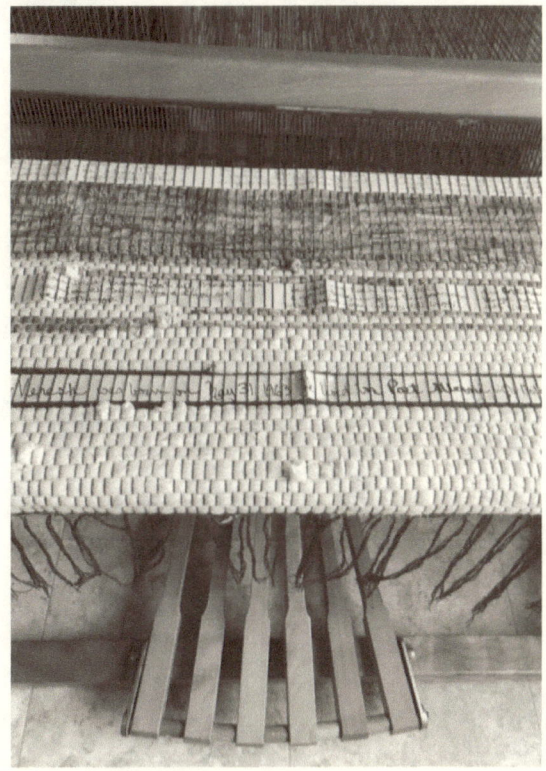

The blanket was now with him and stayed with him through his death and cremation. Though sad indeed, *The Artist* was in a much more grounded and open space than they would have been had the notion of the grieving weaver not been acted on.

Client Two

Another client had suddenly and unexpectedly lost her daughter to a drunk driver who ran her down and killed her. She connected with me, and on our first call, she said that she didn't do "talk therapy." I was at the time a talk therapist. What to do?

As we worked our way through our first call, I discovered that she enjoyed painting. When I asked her if she'd be willing to paint me her grief, she burst into tears and said absolutely.

She began a series of paintings that she titled "Pain Has No Colour." Over eighteen months, she created nine works of art that I would read back to her. It was our agreement that she would paint her feelings to me on canvass and then send me a photo of the artwork. I would then in session put to words the art in front of me so she would know without a doubt that she got her deepest feelings across to me and that I understood the painting. It was important for *The Artist* to know she was understood. It was that very understanding that transformed her grief and enabled her to gradually get back into her life without her sweet daughter.

7. Avoidant Expression—The Filer

The Filer feels at home simply tucking things away in a filing cabinet some-where in their body/mind and imagining they will get back to it later. They seldom do. It's their way of dealing with the overwhelming emotions that often accompany death and loss. Things get filed away, and they move on with their life, truly believing they have dealt with it. It's all neat and tidy and tucked away.

At some point for *The Filer*, the cabinet begins to overflow, and the neat and tidy becomes messy, a bit like Pandora's Box. At this point, *The Filer* usually adopts their second language, which is The Talker, and talk therapy session can begin.

Client Story

I was working with a person who had spent years working in emergency services and had adopted the techniques of *The Filer* as a way to cope with the constant exposure to death and dying. They presented very well, as if they were grounded and together. Initially, it was a bit weird because I knew of their past and all they had witnessed.

I was patient for several sessions, and then one day, I mentioned some of the traits of *The Filer* to them and wondered out loud if they resonated with them. To their surprise and mine, they said, "Yep, that's me. I had tucked all this shit into neat little files and have never gone back to clear them out."

"Would you like to?" I asked.

With a bit of trepidation, they responded, "Yes."

So, *The Filer* and I went into their cabinet and pulled out one file at a time, starting with the easiest file to handle and moving toward the most difficult files. Although the cabinet is not yet empty, they have made great progress and are well on their way into the tough last few files.

Tool Number Two
The All Ready to Go Binder
Getting Your End-of-Life Paperwork Together

What Is an All Ready to Go Binder?

An End-of-Life Binder is a collection place for all your end-of-life paperwork. It can include and is not limited to the following tabs:

1. Last Will and Testament
2. Power of Attorney
3. Representation Agreement
4. Advanced Care Directives
5. Memorial Society Funeral Arrangement Form
6. Celebration of Life Plan
7. Life Insurance Policy Recap
8. Expected Letter of Death in the Home
9. The Digital Me
10. What about My Pets?
11. People to Call List
12. Copies of Personal Identification
13. List of Financial Holdings
14. Last Reviewed Record

By creating your own End-of-Life Binder, you ensure that you and your family are well aware of any and all end-of-life matters that concern your death. The binder is also a conversation piece you can use as a guide as you walk your family through the important end-of-life topics family members need to be aware of well in advance of death. You can use the End-of-Life Planning Checkup as a road map for your binder.

The binder also is a collection point for you and a planning tool that can be revisited on a regular basis to ensure that your plans stay current with your potentially changing wishes.

A copy of your End-of-Life Binder needs to be kept in the home where it is accessible, and an additional copy could be stored with your lawyer, your executor, and/or your children.

You could also link your binder to the green sleeve that we are meant to attach to the right side of our fridge that contains our DNR orders and advanced care directives for easy access in the case of a 911 emergency.

All Ready to Go Binder—How-To Kit
So, let's begin.

Purchase a binder and a package of twelve tabs dividers from Staples. Use the End-of-Life Planning Checkup as a guide and simply start on tab one and work your way through it. As you complete a section of the tab index, file it in the appropriate section of your binder.

Suggestions and Additional Topic Information

1. Last Will and Testament

Why do you need a will and an estate plan? It may not be fun to think about, but after you're gone, you won't have a say in some pretty important matters unless you let your wishes be known. Who will take care of your children? What will happen to your business, your property, or those valuable heirlooms passed down for generations? Here's a link to a helpful article: https://www.equitylawgroup.ca/wills-estate-probate/?gclid=EAIaI QobChMIn8LlnovN8QIVgwh9Ch0qjADnEAAYASAAEgJQ8fD_BwE

2. Power of Attorney

A power of attorney gives your family member the authority to take care of only your financial and legal affairs. This could include paying bills, doing banking, or selling real estate on your behalf. It does not allow him or her to make decisions about your personal or health care. Here's a link you might find helpful: http://seniorsfirstbc.ca/resources/ legal-research-articles/power-of-attorney-article/.

3. Representation Agreement

A Representation Agreement is a document used either for supported or substituted decision-making regarding health care and personal care matters. Often this agreement is combined with the Advanced Care Directives (item 4 below).

Here is a link describing the importance of this document: http://seniors-firstbc.ca/for-professionals/representation-agreements/.

4. Advanced Care Directives

It's important to have a conversation with your loved ones and health care provider about advance care planning while you're healthy. There may be a time when you may not be able to decide for yourself, like when you're very sick or near death, and your loved ones won't know what kind of care you want unless you tell them.

If you are a resident of BC, go to this website for some great information: https://www.doctorsofbc.ca/news/advance-directives.

5. Memorial Society Funeral Arrangement Form

This form, once completed, is kept on file with the Memorial Society in your area. It helps your family know your intended wishes. Please complete and submit this important form AND discuss its contents with your family. If you are a resident of BC, fill out the following form: https://memorialsocietybc.org/PDF/arrange.pdf.

6. Celebration of Life Plan

It's interesting that funerals and celebrations of life have much in common, yet they often appear very different. Each is a ceremony, a gathering of people who share a common loss. But one is more rooted in tradition, while the other is the result of recent changes in social values. Both serve to do three things:

i. Help the bereaved family and their community publicly acknowledge the death of one of their own.
ii. Support the grieving family by surrounding them with caring friends, co-workers, and neighbours.
iii. Move the deceased from one social status to another.

Here's a link to a great checklist: www.tearsofjoyvideo.com/images/how-toplancol.pdf.

7. Life Insurance Policy Recap

Life insurance is not required to pay the debts of the estate. Life insurance proceeds are not part of your estate. They go directly to the beneficiary and are their property. Making a list of your policies and the beneficiaries will help your family manage the non-estate finances that result from your death.

Here's an interesting link to estate law in Canada: http://estatelawcanada. blogspot.com/2011/04/just-what-are-assets-of-estate.html.

8. Expected Letter of Death in the Home

The letter (form) is completed by the patient's physician and sent to the funeral home before the death. This form allows a funeral director to remove a body from a home without pronouncement of death. It's not necessary to call 911.

For resident's of BC, here's a link to the form that you can print off and take to your doctor when the end of life is near: https://www2.gov.bc.ca/ assets/gov/health/forms/3987fil.pdf

9. The Digital Me

Though most people want their digital presence deleted after they die, only 7 per cent have taken the appropriate planning step to ensure their executor has the power to do so. The links below provide useful information on just how you can prepare for the end of your digital life too:

- www.theguardian.com/tv-and-radio/2019/jun/02/ digital-legacy-control-online-identities-when-we-die
- www.pcmag.com/how-to/ how-to-prepare-your-digital-life-for-your-death

10. What about My Pets?

Our pets are family members too and usually end up being well cared for by the family who survive the owner's death. That being said, some careful planning can be done for our pets. The two articles below speak directly to care for our surviving pets:

- www.petsbest.com/blog/what-happens-if-you-pass-away/

- www.petfinder.com/dogs/bringing-a-dog-home/providing-pets-future/

11. People-to-Call List

There are a number of companies and organizations to call, and many of them will require a certificate of death in order to make the changes you need to make. Some of these are:

- BC Hydro or your utilities company
- Your Internet/cable provider, such as Telus, Shaw, or Rogers, to name a few
- Your gas provider, such as Fortis in BC
- Your bank of credit union and your credit card company

Sometimes we have friends and co-workers our family doesn't really know of who are important to us in our work or volunteer circles. Make sure these important people find their way on to the People-to-Call List so they, too, can pay their respects to our deceased loved one. Often a personal call or email will inform the individuals better than an obituary in the local newspaper.

12. Copies of Personal Identification
13. List of Financial Holdings
14. Last Reviewed Record

This is simply a record of when the All Ready to Go Binder was last reviewed to make sure it is still meeting the needs of the family. It's important to go over your end-of-life wishes from time to time just to make sure that what you have written is still what you want.

Tool Number Three
Different Types of Death
And the Grief That Goes with Them

Overview

Some deaths are more challenging to face than others, so this section of the manual, dealing with difficult deaths, is designed to shed some light on the more taboo deaths. We'll explore each uniquely difficult death and look at how the type of death impacts the process of grief. We'll explore how we can learn to work with these challenging deaths in a way that helps people move forward with their grief and reintegrate with life.

Difficult Deaths—Suicide

Suicide is one of the most challenging deaths a person can face. It's mired in mental health issues, shame, guilt, great unknowns, and secrecy. These added dimensions make grief difficult to process within both the family and their community of friends. The grief basket can be full of all manner of emotion, from rage to absolute numbness and everything in between, and it often gets hidden underneath a cone of silence. The book *Silent Grief* by Christopher Lukas and Henry Seiden is an excellent source of helpful information when suicide rears its challenging head.

Difficult Deaths—Drug Overdoses

Drug overdoses are on the rise, especially amongst young people and often with infrequent users. Similar to suicide, deaths by overdose carry social stigma and confusion. Judgement and criticalness show up as well, making the grief process complex and often lonely.

These two difficult deaths, drug overdose and suicide, carry a huge degree of social stigma. If death is taboo, these two deaths are ultra-taboo, often resulting in the survivors being isolated by friends and colleagues who don't know what to say or do, or who have judgements about the manner of death. The book *Silent Grief* speaks to this point of grieving in isolation, where often the family feels as if they're living under a dome of silence. You will also notice more often than not in the obituary the family does not mention how the death occurred, which sets up this kind of untruth that further clouds the grief.

Coupled with the external community reaction to the suicide or drug overdose is all manner of internal questioning and emotional upheaval. All the should haves, could haves, would haves, and what-ifs come up for a look-see. Sadness can be mixed with confusion, anger, numbness, and regret. The grief process is complex and a real emotional roller coaster that more often than not requires some professional support.

Difficult Deaths—Abortion, Miscarriage, Stillbirth, and Infertility

These not-so-visible deaths are a challenge to handle for many reasons and carry some social judgements as well. It can be a lonely time of grief for the woman, even if she's in a committed relationship. It can be difficult for the male partner too. Along with the death of baby is the death of the future that could have been with baby. In the case of infertility, there is no child, but the idea, the dream of being pregnant, giving birth, and having a child dies, and there's a lot of grief associated with that non-death loss that can often be disenfranchised.

Difficult Deaths—MAiD

Medical Assistance in Dying has been available in Canada for four years now and has been understandably controversial. The application process is thorough and must be signed off by two approved doctors. This being said, it is still an unusual death to cope with for friends and families. One of the unusual things is that the death now has a time, a date, and a location, oddly like making a coffee date.

Also, from time to time, there's disagreement amongst family members, some in support of MAiD and others totally against it. It's important that the family has a full and complete conversation about the choice so that all family members have a say and feel included in the decision.

Difficult Deaths—Murder and Accidental Death

These two types of death bring with them unique challenges. Anger, rage, and deep confusion are often present and difficult to deal with. Often in the case of murder, the family pins its hope on the legal system and that a conviction will ease their pain. Most often, 78 per cent of the time, regardless of the legal result, the family runs right into the grief they were avoiding by focusing on the trial.

Accidental deaths often are clouded by confusion and the questions of why. There is no answer to this question, which often sees folks heading down the "why" rabbit hole as opposed to accepting the reality of the loss.

In Summary

Added to these difficult deaths are often considerations such as who died, what was the survivor's relationship with them like, how old was the individual who died, and how old are the survivors. The grief associated with these deaths is often complex and lengthy, regularly requiring the objective and compassionate support of a grief counsellor.

Tool Number Four
Creating Rituals for My Family
Tailor-Made Celebrations

When our first family member died, dear Jody, we didn't do so well with rituals and celebrations. It was new to the current generation of Garretts, and Mom and Dad weren't so good at it back then either. So, we stumbled our way through Jody's end of life.

I remember clearly the year Jody died, especially as we crept toward Christmas. Jody's birthday was December 23, so the holiday season, our first without Jody, was a big deal. I had a hunch we would do our best to deny our way through this first Christmas without her, so I took a risk and had a chat with Mom and Dad. It was a difficult talk for sure, especially for Dad, yet we fumbled our way through it and did come up with a plan for our first Christmas without dear Jody.

We did just a tiny bit better with Dad's death.

But when it came to Peter's dying and death, we seemed to have turned a corner and managed to learn a few helpful things about the end of life. We did a really good job as a family in creating a great goodbye plan that suited our family's needs and values. Peter's dying and ultimately his death was an inspiring catalyst for us all to create meaningful moments, tailor-made family rituals for both ourselves and for Peter's friends and colleagues.

It had been a six-year walk with Peter and his battle against the unrelenting cancer that finally took his life. Our family was exhausted mentally, emotionally, and physically. After Peter's cremation, we all had a chat and decided to have his celebration of life in Whitehorse, Yukon, a year after his death. This would give all of us time to catch our breath, create some space and time, and relax into our new reality without dear brother Peter. It would also give us time to create a celebration of life that reflected the values Peter lived by.

We organized a lovely site right on the banks of the Yukon River, set a date, invited friends and family, and began to create a day for us all to remember Peter. So, a Montreal Canadiens hockey jersey was a mandatory piece of my apparel, which was a Peter request. Actually, demand. We had his playlist, food list, and most importantly, his fun list. We had the urn with his ashes, we had a minister, we had family, we had friends, and we had a beautiful sunny day!

We set up a table in a quiet corner of the hall. On it, we placed a picture of Peter, a large scrapbook, and a bunch of coloured pens and pencils. We popped a sign by the scrapbook that asked people to write something about Peter, to Peter, or for Peter. We were creating a memory book for April and our family while giving folks an opportunity to "visit" with Peter privately that day. The stories and memories were breath-taking and deeply served Mom, who had lost her second child, and April, who had lost her hubby.

The time came for us all to gather by the banks of the Yukon River and witness April releasing Peter's ashes into the river, one last goodbye. As April was pouring Peter into the river, an eagle chased by a crow was flying over-head. Most thought the eagle was Peter; knowing him a little better, I smiled, recognizing him in the crow!

We all returned to the hall and were greeted by a shot glass of Glenfiddich, and at the right time, we all drank a toast to the one and only Peter Eric Garrett.

The important thing about rituals is twofold: they have a spiritual basis or sacredness to them, and they are meaningful to the family mentally, emotion-ally, physically, and spiritually.

Tool Number Five
Before I Go Template

Before I Go

Sharing Gems of My Life's Journey

My Meaningful Moments
What Mattered Most

Before I Go
The Concept
Often, we don't even realize that what we've experienced throughout our lives is of much or any value. We simply write it off as "just our life." Yet when we take time to go through the key moments, the highlights, the memories both good and bad, we discover some meaningful life wisdom imbedded in our stories. A football game with your son, a day at the ocean, a moment with the boss, helping someone out, surviving a tough time, a chance meeting with a stranger—all yield wonderful gems of wisdom if only we look for them.

This workbook is designed to walk you through a process of personal discovery—actually, uncovery. You'll be guided to dig just under the surface of your life for diamonds in the rough, both small and large, that, with a little polish, can be honed into valuable jewels—gems you can leave behind for those you love and predecease. Gems that won't die with you.

The Process
You will be walked through a graceful process that encourages you to slow down a bit, to make some time for yourself to remember and reflect on the

life you've lived to date. You will be led to savour memories of places, people, jobs, times, and events. You'll be encouraged to look at both wins and losses, the good and the bad, and the happy and sad. You'll be encouraged to notice the values and principles you stood by, what you did that worked, and what you did that didn't work so well. All of this contains life lessons you can choose to leave generously behind before you go.

The Steps

The steps you'll follow are described in basic detail below. Have a read through the process first so you can get an idea of what you'll be up to and how the process flows. Read these instructions twice so that you can fully embrace what's required of you, and perhaps you'll formulate a plan for yourself by setting aside time for each step. Don't respond to these instructions until you've read the entire workbook.

Locating the Mine Shaft

A successful mining operation depends on knowing where to drill. In this section, you'll be given areas of your life to drill down into. Complete the questions below:

a. List the ten most influential or important periods of your life and identify those times as work, social, family, or volunteer times.

b. Notice the places you were living during each of these significant timeframes.

c. Identify the year(s) these events took place, when they began, and when they ended.

Noticing Who Was with You

Now that we have the locations established, let's see who was there with you co-creating the events of those times.

a. Make a list of the ten most important people in your life.

b. Link these folks to the ten most important times of your life on your Before I Go table below.

c. Notice if there was a person involved in the event that influenced you but is not on your list of top ten.

d. What role did each person play? Make up titles for them, like good cop, bad cop, instigator, invisible man, etc. Use your imagination to nickname the role they played.

e. What life lesson did you learn from them? List them in point form, and we will explore them more deeply in reflection of the deeper life lessons section.

f. On the chart below list the ten most influential or important periods of your life and identify those times as social (s), family (f), volunteer (v), or work (w) times. Add the place where you were living and, as best as you can, recall the year(s).

	The Event	S	F	V	W	Location	Year(s)	Emotions	Key Word
1									
2									
3									
4									
5									
6									
7									
8									
9									
10									

Discovering What You Felt and What You Learned

Life goes by quickly, and sometimes so quickly that we seldom take time to notice how or what we were feeling. We tend to react so quickly that we don't recognize the emotions we were experiencing. We go straight to expression or suppression. In this step, let's slow it down as you remember the events and play them back in slow motion. Take time to notice what you were feeling. Notice, too, what you were learning.

By each event on your Before I Go table, record up to three emotions you experienced during the event.

In the next column, record a few key words that highlight what you learned.

Reflecting on the Deeper Life Lesson(s)

During this piece of your gems of life walk, you'll be taking a look at the top ten lessons and prioritizing them. Once you have them in order of importance, select the top three and circle them on your Before I Go table.

Sharing Your Learnings in the Form of Stories

Back in the day, elders would teach others by telling stories. We didn't have the multimedia tools then that, to be honest, are a huge distraction for the most part and separate us from spending quality time with our elders. Given that, let's bring this wonderful and graceful way of teaching back to life!

a. Take each of your top three lessons and begin to build a framework for your story. What lesson do you want to share? Who is in the story? How would you begin the story? How would you end it and on what final sentence?

a. Jot your ideas down without editing them, as you would with a brainstorming session.

a. Once you have your notes complete, set them down for a day or two and sleep on them.

a. When you're ready, take your number one item and begin to compose your story. Write like you would speak it. You can even tell your story and record it live first and then transcribe it.

Giving It All Away with Gratitude

Once you have your story book completed, find "gift" times when you can give it away, such as a birthday, Easter, Christmas, an anniversary, or a just because day. Give it to your family member or friend as if it's the most special gift you have ever given them. It is, after all, the gift of you.

The Outcomes

1. An increased sense of self-value

2. An internal feeling of being an elder

3. An overwhelming urge to share your wisdom stories

Tool Number Six
The Grief Tree Project
Bringing Grief Back to Life

The Grief Tree Project
Bringing Grief Back to Life

This manual is all about creating spaces and places for individuals, families, and communities to go when grief comes knocking on our door. In our Western culture, we have banished grief to institutions: hospitals, funeral homes, care homes, and churches. It's as if grief is not welcome in our homes, on our streets, in our neighbourhoods, or in our communities at large.

In banishing grief in this way, we reject one of life's powerful energies—an energy that can inspire, motivate, teach, and birth new life, new ideas, and new projects.

The Grief Tree Project is all about reclaiming grief as a friend, an ally, a companion on whom we can lean. A friend we can count on to lead us into new beginnings and fresh starts. A life force that is necessary for us to truly embrace life fully and live with both passion and purpose.

This manual is designed to support an individual, a family, or a community in bringing grief back into real life, where it so importantly belongs. Grief is not the bad guy, or something to get over or get through. Grief is an inspirational teacher—one we can trust to guide us along life's path.

Acknowledgement

This manual was inspired by my Dene friends who are living with wildfires that have resulted in all of Yellowknife and many communities in the Northwest Territories being evacuated. Their grief, courage, and resilience led me to the create this manual.

In honour of my Dene friends, here is a visual look at how grief began in the NWT, the root causes, how we look at only the branches and leaves, and how we need to dig beneath the soil and extract the roots that have caused the many dysfunctions we experience.

Fanning the flames of the already existing grief is the wildfire situation ripping through the NWT, pouring even more fuel on the fires of grief. It begs the question: How can we use these catastrophic events as inspiration to dig deeper into the historic long-term grief that lives in the Dene peoples? How can we use the current situation, the fires of change, to heal the deeper wounds?

Let's Begin

Let's look at the specific situation of the Dene Nation and how some of their community members have arrived at the place they're at these days. By using these specifics, we will learn how the **Grief Tree** grows and branches onward and upward without us even being conscious of it. From its roots to its leaves, we will unmask the hidden and unexpressed grief in order for us all to be free of the past.

Each individual, each family, each community has its own **Grief Tree** with its own roots, its own trunk, and its own branches. By using the Dene Nation's **Grief Tree** as an example, we will be able to identify our own unique **Grief Tree**.

The Roots

There is more than just one cause of the systemic intergenerational grief carried by many of the Dene Nation's people. It's important to recognize all the interconnected roots that support the **Grief Tree**. Each root needs to be explored and cleared if the branches of grief are to be disempowered. Here are some historic dates and events that have spawned the Dene Nation's **Grief Tree**.

Sixteenth Century: First Contact

European explorers and fur traders began to explore the region then known as North-Western Territory. Martin Frobisher was the first European to make contact in the 1570s.

Seventeenth Century: The Fur Trade

Hudson's Bay Company is granted a commercial trade monopoly.

Colonization: Stolen Lands

Deed of Surrender enacted by the United Kingdom on June 23, 1870.

Treaty #8 signed between the Dene Nations and Government of Canada in June 1899, largest land settlement in Canadian history.

Residential Schools

The first of fourteen residential schools were opened in 1867 by the Catholic Church Grey Nuns; it was called Sacred Heart. The last residential school, Kivalliq Hall, was closed in 1997. Loss of personal agency, individuality, spirituality, and community were some of the direct results of life in residential schools.

The Branches Get Our Attention

These branches are important to look at and handle, for sure. Although they are the presenting issue, it is not the end of the work at hand. Once we've made progress on the presenting issues listed below, we have then created both space and energy to dig more deeply into the root causes, the events that spawned these behaviours in the first place. While reading through this section, refer to the **Dene Grief Tree** on the following page.

Fear, scarcity, neglect, and abuse (physical, mental, sexual, and spiritual) all gang up with the loss of self-esteem and self-worth some Dene community members have experienced. The environment many Dene children grew up in, described above, has resulted in the many behaviours that are portrayed in the branches of the **Dene Grief Tree**.

Addictions, suicides, drug overdose deaths, and murders are some of the behaviours that are acted out and are the direct result of historical, generational, family, community, and environmental grief.

The Dene Grief Tree

The Grief Tree

LOSS of SELF ESTEEM & SELF WORTH

DISORDERS

SUICIDE & DRUG OVERDOSE DEATH

FEAR & SCARCITY

ABUSE & NEGLECT

ADDICTIONS

SOIL IS OUR SPIRITUALITY

THE TRUNK OF LOSSES

Traditional Language
Dress
Food
Family
Community

Spirituality
Home
Way of life
Personal Agency

FIRST CONTACT 16TH CENTURY

FUR TRADE 17TH CENTURY

COLONIZATION, STOLEN LANDS

RESIDENTIAL SCHOOL

LOSS OF AGENCY

THE ROOTS ARE NOT US!

A Personal Example

Following up the **Dene Nations Grief Tree** example, here is my personal **Grief Tree**. I share it with you so that you get an idea of how personal our own **Grief Tree** can be. Notice the events that are the roots of my personal unexpressed grief, and notice the branches of my tree to see how the unexpressed grief turned into not-so-healthy habits of my life.

Stephen's Grief Tree

Job Changes 5 year Intervals

Anger Outburst

Few Friendships

Divorces

Emotionally Unavailable

SOIL IS OUR SPIRITUALITY

THE BARK
I'm not good enough.
I'm not lovable.
I'm not invisible.
I don't matter.

Grandpa Joe's Death

Emotionally Distant Father

Dad Stops The Breast Feeding

Unmet Needs Eldest of 5

THE ROOTS ARE NOT US!

The Grief Tree Growth Process

1. As an Individual

As an individual, there are several ways we can approach creating our own personal **Grief Tree**. We can look at our behaviours in life, especially those that tend to get us into difficulties with family, relationships, friends, and co-workers. Here are several questions to ask yourself:

- What are some things I do unconsciously that cause distance or upset?
- What are some things I do unconsciously that are not good for my mental, emotional, or physical health?
- What are some habits I have that I don't even recognize as habits?
- What are some things I did around others that didn't work for them?
- When my emotions are big, what do I usually do with them?
- When others are experiencing big emotions, what do I typically do?

You can also start to explore your family life from as far back as you can remember and see what kind of "training" around dying, death, and grief you received as a child.

- How did your family respond when a favourite pet died?
- What happened when a loved one died?
- How did your parents express their grief?
- What was going on in the world when you were a child? Was there a war? A recession?
- What was television teaching you? What shows did you watch?

Another way in is to explore your own personal relationship with death and grief.

- If death and grief were friends of yours, how would you describe your relationship with them?
- When you think of your own mortality, what thoughts and emotions come up for you?
- When you think of a loved one of yours dying, what happens for your internally?

As you work through these different thought processes, make notes in your journal and track your findings. Start to formulate a clear picture of your relationship with dying, death, and grief. Then wonder the following:

- What are the roots causes of my dysfunctional relationship with death and grief?
- How did I create such an unworkable relationship with death?
- Where did this nonsense come from in the first place?

My Own Personal Grief Tree

My Personal
Grief Tree

MY TRUNK OF LOSSES

SOIL IS OUR SPIRITUALITY

THE ROOTS ARE NOT US!

2. As a Family

Go through a similar process with your family of origin. Get curious about what was going on inside your family while you were growing up.

Check things out with your siblings, with your mom and dad. Wonder and learn how your family handled dying, death, grief, and loss.

3. As a Community

Next, have a look at what was going on in and around you historically in your home town. Same questions apply to your community relationships. What was your outside world teaching you about dying, death, grief, and loss? The newspapers, the radio shows, television, and movies train us to approach dying, death, and grief a certain way. What way was that for you?

Now for the Grief Tree

Once you've taken a close look at all these places, spaces, and questions, you'll begin to notice the behaviours you act out in order to protect yourself from dying, death, and grief. You'll begin to notice where these behaviours are rooted, and you'll understand the beliefs you made up about yourself to make the whole **Grief Tree** grow and evolve into your own personal tree. Then simply name the roots, name the trunk of beliefs, and name the dysfunctional behaviour branches. Once done, you can now begin to renovate your tree from the roots to the branches. Here is one way you can approach it.

A Way through the Tangles of the Grief Tree
Grief, Gratitude, and Growth

Grief

In our North American death-denying culture, we kick grief to the back corner of the darkest closet we can find. Grief is not welcome, and when it is present, we're expected to get over it within days. This is how grief is currently handled, but it doesn't make it right. It's time to reinvent how we process grief.

Grief is a natural human response to change, loss, and death. If we have loved something, somewhere, or someone, we'll feel grief in our hearts; grief is simply love turned inside out.

When we choose to lean into our grief, to express our grief in healthy ways, and to reach out for support, we will find our way through.

I had no idea what to do when Jody died, as it was my first family death. Thankfully, a friend of a friend was a spiritual grief counsellor and saved my butt! Though my grief over Jody's death was intense, my counsellor and I found many creative and helpful ways to express it, work with it, and move through it. Six months later, I was in pretty good shape with my grief journey. Here are several helpful hints I picked up on how to process grief in a healthy way that will result in a sense of grief being received, relieved, and released.

✓ Grief requires a village of support.
✓ Sometimes we need professional grief support for a while.
✓ There is everything right about grieving in healthy ways.
✓ Grief is a unique journey, and we each speak our grief in our own language.
✓ Grief is an active process and requires our participation.
✓ Grief is a reflection of our love.
✓ Grief requires a sender and a receiver.

Once our grief has been expressed and processed and we have moved forward with it, and once it has been accepted and validated by at least one other person, we will find gratitude knocking on our door.

Gratitude

Once grief has been well expressed and well received, an odd thing can happen for us grievers: gratitude can show up! I know, it surprised me too, and for a while, it didn't make any sense to me. What was there to be grateful about? Well, let me explain.

Shakespeare once said, "Parting is such sweet sorrow." He wrote this sentence while experiencing the grief resulting from the death of his son. Notice the use of the word *sweet*. For me, this sweetness is actually gratitude. I remember saying goodbye to my dear brother, Peter, for the last time. He was on his deathbed and hours from taking his last breath. He wanted only his wife, April, present for his death, so I was making my leave. I kissed him on the forehead one last time and said, "See you next time, dear brother."

I turned to walk out the door, and before leaving the room, I looked back for one last time. In that moment, I was struck by Shakespeare's words. I felt a profound sweetness and, right beside it, a deep sorrow. The sweetness was about how grateful I was that Peter's suffering would soon cease. The sweetness was about how grateful I was to have known him.

Yes, gratitude!

As I look closely at all the other deaths I have experienced, the sweetness/gratitude was there in each and every one of them, without fail. This feeling of gratitude helped me to make meaning of the life my loved one had lived. It was the fertilizer that helped me grow and evolve into the person I am today.

Yes, gratitude.

Growth

Once we've done a fair bit of healthy grieving and stumbled into our own sense of gratitude, we can then move into this place of using our grief and gratitude for our personal spiritual growth. Yes, dying, death, and grief can indeed turn into compost for our own spiritual growth. In fact, death is actually the very best teacher on good old planet Earth.

Once we've processed a fair bit of our grief and have tasted the sweetness of gratitude for the death of our loved one, we can then start to look for the inspiration the death has gifted us with. We can start to look for those values our loved one carried. We can start to hear and understand the story of our loved one's life and mine it for the gems of wisdom our loved left behind in their stories. We can begin to let the loss and the grief and the gratitude grow us.

Here's an example from my own life:

My brother's death-bed regrets were, in fact life, lessons for me.

Creating Spaces for the Grief Tree

The **Grief Tree** could be an actual place in community where people gather to express their grief, to be together in their sadness, and to then move forward toward a new normal. It could also be a space in the local schools, either inside or outside the classroom. It could be a place in the family yard where a tree for a loved one is planted. It could be a space in the family home, with a plant placed in a special memory corner. What could a **Grief Tree** space look and feel like in the home, the garden, the community, or the school classroom?

Helpful Resources

Stuck in the Grief Mud?

Some Steps to Move Forward in Life

Understand why we get stuck, and then intend to move ahead in life.
Handle the basics: food, exercise, companionship, and sleep.
Get back to a daily routine and step out of those temporary bad habits.
Discover your own brand of spirituality and live it.
Reclaim your own self-worth.
Turn on your inspiration.

Eight Useful Tools to Deal with Dying and Death

1. An Open Heart

This is an important tool not only to help in the dying process but also to have in your living process. To have an open heart to me means coming to a situation or person with no preconceived ideas or judgements.

2. Compassion

To have compassion for another is to be able to have a deep awareness of the suffering of another and to want to try to help relieve that suffering in whatever way possible.

3. Empathy

To have empathy for another means that you are able to identify with what they are going through, put yourself in their shoes, and share their emotions.

4. Respect

To be respectful of another is to understand that their choices are their own and it is not our place to judge others. We are all individuals with individual ideas and ways of life.

5. Encouragement

I think encouragement is a good thing to bring to the table when helping others. This is their journey, and they do have a say in things that they would like to see happen. Encouragement is also a good thing for the family caring for someone who is dying, to let them know that what they're feeling is okay.

6. Acceptance

To have acceptance is to be open to different beliefs and traditions, and to just be accepting of where everyone is at the time when you're there to try and help them. Accept them for who they are and where they are on their journey.

7. Understanding/Open Mind

I think if you can come to the situation with understanding of what the family and the dying loved one is going through, it can be very helpful. Being able to understand all of the emotions that arise in a situation where a loved one is dying is a gift. Everyone's journey is different, so it is very important to have an open mind.

8. Kindness

Kindness is a must, not just when someone is dying, but in everyday life. If you can come to someone with kindness in your heart, then doors will open and healing will happen.

THE LANGUAGES & SUGGESTED ACTIVITIES
Created by Stephen Garrett, MA

THE TALKER
Talk therapy, walk and talk session in nature, community/support groups

THE WRITER
Journaling, poetry, writing a letter to someone, starting a blog, social media posts

THE FILER
Working on one thing at a time, keep it simple and organised until they feel ready to explore the other possible languages they have

THE SENSITIVE
Playing music, singing, creative expression, spoken word poetry

7 Languages of Sorrow

THE ARTIST
Painting, drawing, sculpting, baking, weaving, knitting, carving

THE SEEKER
Ritual, ceremony, prayer, meditation

THE MOVER
Dancing, exercise, hiking, breathwork, yoga

Questions to Ask:
What do you like to do in your spare time?
Do you have any hobbies?
Do you consider yourself to be a creative person?
What does your spiritual practice look like?
Do you enjoy the outdoors/being in nature?
What does your self care look like?
What do you and your friends like to do for fun?
What do your Friday nights look like?
How often do you like to read/write?

Designed by Haley Jane & Jade Mathiscyk

111

Afterwords

Stephen's Grief Philosophy

In the front entry of my home, we have a barrel that holds umbrellas and walking sticks because you never know when you'll need one or the other here on Canada's unpredictable West Coast. They are simply available to anyone who needs them.

In my work with grieving clients, I often refer to myself as Grief's Walking Stick, a handy fella to have around just in case the grief journey gets a little bumpy. My clients and I walk together along their grief path, and from time to time, they pick up their Grief Walking Stick for support during the particularly challenging times. Other times, we simply walk along together and review their progress and prepare for what's next on their horizon.

As a counsellor, I ought not be careless and create a dependency on myself as my clients' only grief resource. Personally, I am committed to helping them use the resources they already have in place—their own life's wisdom, family members, and friends—more than relying solely on an expert, me, to get them through. Yet I know from time to time, they will require the support and guidance from someone who has walked along grief's path and knows the way and how to negotiate those particularly tight corners. So, just in case, their Grief Walking Stick is available, and that in and of itself is a huge comfort.

Over time, clients learn to use their walking stick when they need it most, for those particularly rocky times. Otherwise, they build their own grief supports within their family and community, leaving their Grief Walking Stick for others more in need.

Grief's Walking Stick is all about building grief-resilient individuals, families, and ultimately communities. Secondarily, it focuses on rebranding death and grief from the ill-informed concept of the Grim Reaper to a new model—the Inspirational Teacher—an approach that will support folks in turning toward their grief and loss as opposed to turning away from it, as is so often the case here in death- and grief-denying North America.